M. (Moses) Mielziner

The Jewish Law Of Marriage And Divorce In Ancient And Modern Times

M. (Moses) Mielziner

The Jewish Law Of Marriage And Divorce In Ancient And Modern Times

ISBN/EAN: 9783742845177

Manufactured in Europe, USA, Canada, Australia, Japa

Cover: Foto ©Lupo / pixelio.de

Manufactured and distributed by brebook publishing software (www.brebook.com)

M. (Moses) Mielziner

The Jewish Law Of Marriage And Divorce In Ancient And Modern Times

THE JEWISH LAW

OF

MARRIAGE AND DIVORCE

IN ANCIENT AND MODERN TIMES,

AND

ITS RELATION TO THE LAW OF THE STATE,

BY

REV. DR. M. MIELZINER,
Professor of the Talmud and of the Rabbinical Disciplines at the Hebrew Union College.

THE BLOCH PUBLISHING AND PRINTING COMPANY,
CINCINNATI, 1884.

Entered according to Act of Congress, in the year 1884, by
The BLOCH Publishing and Printing Company,
in the Office of the Librarian of Congress at Washington.

INSCRIBED TO

THE BLESSED MEMORY OF

MY BELOVED FATHER AND TEACHER,

Rev. BENJAMIN MIELZINER,

Late Rabbi in Schubin, Germany,

IN FILIAL PIETY,

> The Author.

PREFACE.

In more than one respect, the subject treated in the following book deserves a full share of our attention. Regarded merely from the general scientific point of view, and especially from that of the history of law and of comparative legislation, it must be of the greatest interest to obtain a clear insight into a very minute and circumstantial law of marriage, the origin of which dates back to Biblical antiquity, and which, although adapted in many particulars to conditions that have since changed, nevertheless has a well-founded historical importance, from the fact that, through a long succession of centuries, it has exerted the most salutary influence upon the domestic life of the Jewish people all over the world.

This law of marriage, however, lays claim to more than a mere historical and archæological interest, inasmuch as it affects the life of to-day. In numerous instances it is still acknowledged as the rule and criterion of practical conduct. Many of its precepts and regulations are authoritative for religious Israelites even where, as here in the United States and in some European countries, civil marriage exists and the State takes no cognizance whatever of the ecclesiastical element of marriage. In those countries in which the law is adapted to the different forms of faith of the recognized religious bodies, and where consequently the Jews have also their own jurisdiction in matrimonial affairs, as is the case, for instance, in Russia, Poland and partially also in Austria, Hungary, and other States, Jewish marriages are contracted and dissolved essentially solely in accordance with the ordinances of the Jewish Marriage Law.

In consideration of the importance of the subject in question, the RABBINICAL LITERARY ASSOCIATION OF AMERICA, at a meeting held in DETROIT, MICH., in the year 1880, declared, "that an exhaustive presentation of the historical and literary material bearing upon the Jewish Laws of Marriage and Divorce is very desirable," and a commission was appointed "to collect that material and to report thereon at one of the following meetings of this Association." [1] At the meeting held in CHICAGO the following year the committee requested and was allowed further time for report. Since then there has been no opportunity for presenting such report, for the reason that the Association, since the lamented death of its founder and President, the Rev. Dr. M. LILIENTHAL, seems to have lost its vitality. As chairman of the above-mentioned committee, I have nevertheless not neglected to give the subject my fullest attention. The rich material collected through a careful study of the sources, and by an investigation of the modern literature of the subject, I have elaborated into a course of lectures "On the Jewish Law of Marriage and Divorce," which I have delivered to the Senior Class of the Hebrew Union College. The essential part of these lectures, considerably expanded, and with the addition of numerous notes and references to the sources, is here presented to the reading public.

The author indulges in the hope that this treatise will not only be welcome to ministers of congregations and jurists,

---

[1] Report of the Proceedings of the Second Regular Meeting of the Rabbinical Literary Association, published in the *Hebrew Review*, vol. I., p. 86, *et seq.*

but will also furnish not uninteresting reading for the educated public in general.

With the exception of an *excursus* in Dr. M. KALISCH's Commentary on Leviticus, which, treating of the Mosaic Marriage Law, pays also some attention to the rabbinical regulations, and of Dr. GINSBURG's article on Marriage, in Kitto's Cyclopædia, adopted also in Clintock and Strong's Cyclopædia of Biblical Literature, nothing, so far as I know, has been published in English on this subject. In German there are some few able treatises, particularly one by the late Dr. Z. FRANKEL, (¹) and one by the late Rabbi LEOPOLD LOEW, (²) to which I have occasionally referred in the notes. The present work differs from them, however, not only in the systematic arrangement and popular treatment of the material, but also in the special notice which it takes of all the questions which have arisen in modern times, concerning the Jewish Law of Marriage, and of all the resolutions which have been passed in the last forty years by the various Rabbinical Conferences and Synods for the purpose of bringing some of the provisions of the Jewish marriage law into harmony with the changed circumstances of our time. For the first time, these important resolutions, which are scattered in the reports of the respective sessions, have been collected, and are given *verbatim* in their appropriate connection.

(¹) *Grundlinien des mosaisch-talmudischen Eherechts*, vom Director Dr. Z. FRANKEL. Breslau, 1860.

(²) *Eherechtliche Studien*, von LEOPOLD LOEW, published in the periodical *Ben Chananja*, vol. III.–V.

Of other treatises on this subject we mention the following:

SAALSCHUETZ, *Mosaisches Recht*. Berlin, 1853 (sec. edition), chapters 102–106.

FASSEL, *Das Mosaisch-rabbinische Civilrecht*. Wien, 1852, I , pp. 28–71.

LICHTSCHEIN, *Die Ehe nach Talmudischer Auffassung* Leipzig, 1879

Besides, M. DUSCHAK published a book—*Das Mosaisch-Talm. Eherecht*, which, however, I never had the opportunity to get a sight of.

Moreover, in the notes, proper attention has been paid to the provisions of the Common Law and of the laws of the various States of the Union on the subject, so that the relation of the Jewish law to the law of the land is in some cases more clearly exhibited. Only works which are recognized as authorities in America have been referred to, namely, Kent's Commentaries, Bouvier's Institutes, and especially Bishop on Marriage and Divorce.

Before setting forth at length the essential laws concerning marriage, a chapter has been introduced on the ethical doctrines of the Bible and the Talmud concerning this relation, since, in practice, these doctrines have mitigated the severity of many of the provisions of the law, and have substantially contributed to make the Jewish marriage, in all times and countries, a shining example of chastity, devotion and domestic bliss, so that it has not infrequently been set up as a model by the adherents of other faiths.

THE AUTHOR.

Cincinnati, August, 1884.

TABLE OF CONTENTS.

	PAGE.
INTRODUCTION.	13

CHAPTER I.

THE MARRIAGE RELATION, ACCORDING TO THE ETHICAL DOCTRINES OF THE BIBLE AND THE TALMUD. §§ 1, 2	15

CHAPTER II.

THE SOURCES OF THE JEWISH MARRIAGE LAW. § 3.	20
Modern Modifications. § 4.	22

CHAPTER III.

LEGAL VIEW OF MARRIAGE. § 5.	25

CHAPTER IV.

MONOGAMY AND POLYGAMY.

a. Biblical and Talmudical Period. § 6.	28
b. Rabbinical Interdiction of Polygamy. § 7.	30
c. Circumstances Influencing the Prevalence of Monogamy. § 8.	31

PROHIBITED MARRIAGES.

CHAPTER V

A. CONSANGUINITY AND AFFINITY. § 9.	33
a. Biblical Degrees. § 10	34
b. Talmudical Extensions. § 11.	37
c. Not Objectionable Degrees. § 12.	39
TABLE OF PROHIBITED DEGREES.	41

CHAPTER VI.

B. PROHIBITION IN CONSIDERATION OF CHASTITY.

 I. The Divorced Wife. § 13. — — — — 42
 II. The Adulterers. § 14. — — — — 42
 III Suspicion. § 15. — — — — 43
 IV. *Mamzer.* § 16. — — — — 43
 V. Spadones. § 17. — — — — 44

CHAPTER VII.

C. PROHIBITIONS ON ACCOUNT OF RELIGIOUS AND OTHER CONSIDERATIONS.

 1. Intermarriage.
  a. Biblical and Talmudical Grounds. § 18 — — 45
  b. The Question of Intermarriage in Modern Times. § 19. 47
  c. Further Opinions on the subject of Intermarriage. § 20. 49
  d. Conclusion. § 21. — — — — 52
 2. Levirate and Chalitza.
  a. Biblical and Talmudical Precept. § 22. — — 54
  b. Modern Views and Resolutions of Rabbinical Conferences. § 23. — — — — — 57
 3. Prohibitions Especially for Aaronites. § 24. — — 59

CHAPTER VIII.

TEMPORARY IMPEDIMENTS.

 I. Preventive Against Uncertainty of Paternity. § 25. — 61
 II. Pregnancy and the Suckling Child. § 26. — — 62
 III. Mourning. § 27. — — — — 63
 IV. Obstructive Days. § 28. — — — — 63

CHAPTER IX.

QUALIFICATIONS TO CONTRACT MARRIAGE.

 1. Consent.
  a. Mutual Consent, § 29. — — — — 66
  b. Conditional Consent. § 30. — — — 67
  c. Error and False Representation. § 31. — — 69
  d. Consent of Parents. § 32. — — — 69
 2. Mental Capacity.
  a. Idiocy and Lunacy. § 33. — — — 70
  b. The Deaf and Dumb. § 34. — — — 70
 3. Legal Age.
  a. At what Age Marriage is Lawful. § 35. — — 71
  b. The Minor Daughter. § 36. — — — 72

THE FORM OF CONCLUDING MARRIAGE.

CHAPTER X.

THE FORM OF MARRIAGE IN ANCIENT TIMES.

Introductory. § 37. - - - - - - 75
  A. *Betrothment.*
    a. Its Term and Nature. § 38. - - - 76
    b. The Modes by which Betrothment was Effected § 39. 77
    c. Betrothal through Representatives. § 40. - - 80
    d. Witnesses. § 41. - - - - - 80
    e. Doubtful Betrothment. § 42. - - - 81
    f. Benediction of Betrothal § 43. - - - 82
  B. *Nuptials.*
    a. Interval between the two Acts. § 44. - - 82
    b. Term and Essence of the Ceremonies. § 45. - 83
    c. Religious Ceremonies. § 46 - - - 84
    d. Combination of Betrothal and Nuptials. § 47. - 85
    e. Kethuba. § 48. - - - - - 85
    f. Form of the Kethuba. § 49. - - - 87
    g. Former Importance of the Kethuba. § 50. - 88

CHAPTER XI

THE FORM OF MARRIAGE IN OUR TIME
  1. *The Modern Mode of Solemnization.* § 51. - - 90
    Minor Differences. § 52. - - - - 91
    a. One or Two Wedding Rings. - - - 91
    b. The Formula of the Wedding Ceremony. - 92
    c. The Ritual. - - - - - 93
  2 *Civil Marriage.* § 53. - - - - - 93

THE EFFECTS OF MARRIAGE.

CHAPTER XII.

THE OFFSPRING OF LAWFUL AND UNLAWFUL MARRIAGES.
Rabbinical Principles and Rules. § 54 - - - 95

CHAPTER XIII

HUSBAND AND WIFE.
Introductory. § 55. - - - - - - 98
  1. *Marital Duties and Rights.*
    a. The Husband's Duties. § 56. - - - 98
    b. His Legal Rights. § 57. - - - 102
    c. The Wife's Duties and Rights. § 58 - - 103
  2. *The Wife's Property.* § 59 - - - - 104

DISSOLUTION OF MARRIAGE.

CHAPTER XIV.

DISSOLUTION BY DEATH.

Introductory. § 60. - - - - - - 108
   a. The Evidence of Death. § 61. - - - - 109
   b. The Witnesses to the Death. §62. - - - 110
   c. Consequences of a Premature Remarriage. § 63. - 111
   d. Identification. § 64. - - - - - 112
   e. Absent and not heard of. § 65. - - - 112
   f. Resolutions of Rabbinical Conferences. § 66. - 113

CHAPTER XV.

DIVORCE.

1. Introductory. § 67. - - - - - - 115
2. Regulations of the Mosaic Law. § 68. - - - 116
3. Rabbinical Interpretation and Provisions. § 69. - 118
4. Restriction of the Right of Divorce. § 70. - - 120
5. Specific Causes for Divorce.
   a. Mutual Agreement. § 71. - - - - 121
   b. The Husband's Causes. § 72. - - - 122
   c. The Wife's Causes. § 73. - - - - 123
   d. Divorce Against the Will of Both Parties. § 74. 124
6. Causes for Divorce considered in Modern Legislation. § 75. 125
7. The Bill of Divorce. § 76. - - - - - 128
8. Form of the Bill of Divorce. § 77. - - - - 129

CHAPTER XVI.

THE JEWISH LAW OF DIVORCE IN MODERN TIMES.

   a. A Modern Question and its attempted solution. § 78. - 130
   b. Propositions submitted to the Philadelphia Conference. § 79. - - - - - - - - 132
   c. Resolutions passed by that Conference. § 80. - 135
   d. Explanatory Remarks to those Resolutions. § 81. - 136
   e. Conclusion. § 82. - - - - - - 137

ALPHABETICAL INDEX, - - - - - - - 139

THE JEWISH LAW

OF

MARRIAGE AND DIVORCE.

INTRODUCTION.

MARRIAGE is the most important and sacred of all domestic relations. It is the origin of all other relations of life, and forms the foundation of human society. Besides, it is a relation in which man's happiness for life is materially involved, and which serves to protect and promote moral purity.

In Israel, marriage has at all times been regarded in this light, as is already evident from the prominence which is given to it in Biblical and post-Biblical literature. Many chapters and innumerable passages of Scripture speak of this relation, and no less than five treatises of the Talmud are almost exclusively devoted to regulations concerning husband and wife.

But with regard to those relations of life, including marriage, which are regulated in the Bible and in the Talmud, a distinction should be made between ETHICAL DOCTRINES and LAWS.

Ethical doctrines teach the eternal principles of justice, love, and moral purity, as a standard of duty and a model of perfection. Law is the embodiment of these principles, their application to and modification in certain relations, under existing circumstances. Ethical doctrines regard man as an individual created in the image of God, and destined to happiness and perfection. Law regards man as a member of human society and a subject of a certain state or government, and its main object is to protect that society and secure its welfare. Ethical doctrines appeal to man's reason, heart and will; law regulates his actions. Obedience to ethical doctrines is a matter of CONSCIENCE. Obedience to laws is enforced by penalties. Ethical doctrines are uncompromising. They protest against all existing evils of human society, and tell man what he ought to be, and how his relations ought to be ordered according to the will of God. Laws consider man as he is, and his relations as they are, and try to diminish and restrict general evils which under existing circumstances can not at once be abolished and extirpated.

The Bible contains laws as well as ethical doctrines. The former are laid down in the second, third and fourth books of the Pentateuch (namely, Exodus, chapters xx.-xxiii.; chapters xxv.-xxxi.; chapters xxxiv. and xxxv.; Leviticus, chapters i.-viii.; xi.-xxv., xxvii.; Numbers, chapters v.-x.; xviii., xix.; xxvii.-xxx.) and, with some modifications, are repeated in Deuteronomy, chapters iv.-xxvi. As all laws contained in these books of Moses are proclaimed in the name of God, who is the source of all ethical truth, it is but natural that even this legal part of Scripture is occasionally blended with ethical doctrines and principles. The prophetical, poetical and didactical books, to which also the first chapters of Genesis belong, contain ethical teachings only.

As the Bible, so also the Talmud, contains both laws and ethical doctrines. The interpretation and development of the law is the object of the HALACHA, while the ethical doctrines and views belong to the province of the AGADA.

CHAPTER I.

THE MARRIAGE RELATION, ACCORDING TO THE ETHICAL DOCTRINES OF THE BIBLE AND THE TALMUD.

§ 1.

THE ethical view of the Pentateuch concerning marriage is indicated in the following passage in the history of man's creation:

"And the Lord said, It is not good that man should be alone; I will make him a helpmate for him.

"He made a woman, and brought her unto the man.

"And Adam said, This is now bone of my bone, and flesh of my flesh; she shall be called Woman, because she was taken out of Man.

"Therefore shall a man leave his father and his mother, and cleave unto his wife, and they shall be one flesh." (Gen. ii. 18–24.)

To this must be added, from chapter i. 28:

"And God blessed them and said to them, Be fruitful, and multiply, and fill the earth and subdue it."

The principles expressed in these passages are:

1. Marriage is a divine institution for man's happiness and welfare.
2. Woman is a part of man's own being; hence, not, as according to the degrading views of almost all nations of antiquity, his inferior and slave, but equal to him in dignity, and destined to be a help at his side.

3. Through mutual, sincere affection, which is even more intensive than that which naturally exists between children and their parents, husband and wife shall become one flesh, that is, they shall coalesce in one being, one person.

4. Marriage was ordained and blessed by God, not only for the purpose of securing the material and moral welfare of the individual, but also to preserve and continue the human race.

The consequences of these principles are:

(*a*) As a divine institution, marriage must be sacred and inviolable.

(*b*) Perfect union and harmony shall exist between husband and wife; in mutual love and affection they shall assist each other, contribute to each other's perfection and happiness, and share a common destiny as to the good or evil which shall happen to them.

(*c*) The principle that "man shall cleave TO HIS wife, and that they shall become one being," excludes Polygamy as well as Divorce, as contravening the will of God and the design of marriage.

(*d*) The double purpose of marriage to secure the welfare of the individual and preserve and propagate the human race, implies the duty of man toward himself and to human society to leave the state of singleness and enter the state of married life, as soon as he is able to found and support a family.

The same sublime principles concerning the conjugal relation pervade the other ethical books of Scripture, especially the book of Proverbs:

"Whoso findeth a wife findeth a good thing, and obtaineth favor of the Lord." (xviii. 22.)

"House and riches are the inheritance of fathers, and a prudent wife is from the Lord." (xix. 14.)

"A virtuous woman is a crown to her husband." (xii. 4.)

The last chapter of Proverbs contains a glorious alphabetical song in praise of the noble wife, beginning with the words:

"Whoso findeth a virtuous wife, findeth that her price is far above rubies."

"She doeth him good and not evil all the days of her life." (xxxi. 10–12.)

The same book is profuse in warnings against any violation of the purity and sanctity of the conjugal relation (ii. 16–19; v. 8–22; vi. 24–35; vii. 5–27, and other passages). On the other hand, the purity of marriage life is recommended and its happiness praised in the following figure:

"Drink waters out of thine own cistern, and refreshing waters out of thine own well.

"Let them be only thine own, and not strangers with thee.

"Let thy fountain be blessed, and rejoice with the wife of thy youth.—Be thou ravished always with her love." (vs. 15–19.)

Similar, also, is the admonition in the book of Ecclesiastes:

"Live joyfully with the wife whom thou lovest." (ix. 6.)

The discourses of the Prophets very often refer to the conjugal relation. The sacredness of this relation is there repeatedly used as a figure to symbolize that relationship which subsists between God and his people. Thus, Hosea ii. 21, 22, represents the Lord as concluding a covenant with Israel, saying:

"And I will betroth thee unto me forever.

"I will betroth thee unto me in righteousness, and in judgment, and in loving kindness, and in mercies.

"I will betroth thee unto me in faithfulness."

Malachi speaks more directly about marriage when he terms it a covenant, concluded in the presence of God, who looks with anger upon the treachery of faithlessness, and in whose eyes divorce is hateful:

"The Lord has been witness between thee and the wife of thy youth, against whom thou hast dealt treacherously; yet is she thy companion, and the wife of thy covenant. * * * * Therefore take heed to your spirit, and let none deal treacherously against the wife of his youth.

"For the Lord, the God of Israel, saith that he hateth dismissal." (ii. 14–17.)

§ 2.

The sublime ethical doctrines of the Bible concerning the matrimonial relation are re-echoed also in the Rabbinical sayings contained in the Talmud and Midrash. The following is a selection from these sayings:

"He who liveth without a wife is no perfect man." (Yebamoth 63.)

"To be unmarried is to live without joy, without blessing, without kindness, without religion, without protection, without peace." (Yebamoth 62.)

"As soon as a man marries, his sins decrease." (Yebamoth 63.)

"First build a house and plant a vineyard (i. e., provide for the means of the household) and then take a wife." (Sota 24.)

"No man without a wife, neither a woman without a husband, nor both of them without God" (Bereshith Rabba, chap. 8.)

"If virtuous, they are helpmates to each other; if not, they stand against each other." (Yebamoth 63.)

"God dwells with the faithful husband and wife. Without him they are consumed by the fire of strife." (¹) (Sota 17.)

(¹) This sentence contains, in the original, an inimitable play on words. The word איש ("Ish," the husband) and אשה ("Isha," the wife) have

"Descend a step in choosing a wife." (Yebamoth 63.)

"Let youth and old age not be joined in marriage, lest the purity and peace of domestic life be disturbed." (Sanhedr. 76; Yebamoth 101.)

"He who marries for money, his children shall be a curse to him." (Kidd. 70.)

"A man's home means his wife." (Yoma 2.)

"Let a man be careful to honor his wife, for he owes to her alone all the blessing of his house." (B. Metzia 59.)

"If in anger the one hand removed thy wife, let the other hand again bring her to thy heart." (Sanhedrin 107b.)

"A man should be careful lest he afflict his wife, for God counts her tears." (B. Metzia 59.)

"Honor thy wife, and thou wilt be happy." (B. Metzia 59.)

"Who is rich? He who has a noble wife." (Sota 17.)

"Love your wife like yourself, honor her more than yourself: you will then see the fulfillment of the promise: 'And thou shalt know that there is peace in thy tent.'" (Yebamoth 63.)

"If thy wife is small, bend down to her, to take counsel from her." (B. Metzia 59.)

"Tears are shed on God's altar for the one who forsakes the love of his youth." (Gittin 90.)

"He who divorces his wife is hated before God." (Gittin 90.)

"He who sees his wife die, has, as it were, been present at the destruction of the temple." (Sanhedrin 22.)

"The whole world is darkened for him whose wife died in his lifetime." (Sanhedrin 29.)

"A husband's death is felt by none as by his wife. A wife's death is felt by none as by her husband." (Sanhedrin 22.)

---

the letters *Aleph* and *Shin* in common, to which the letters *Yod* and *He* are respectively added. These two additional letters form the name of God, יה ("Yah"). If this name of God is taken from the faithless husband and wife, then only אש ("Esh," fire) remains on either side, indicating that the mutual fire of passion and strife will surely consume them.

CHAPTER II.

THE SOURCES OF THE JEWISH MARRIAGE LAW.

§ 3.

The main sources of the Jewish Marriage Law are the provisions of the Mosaic code embodied in the Pentateuch, and those which are laid down in the Talmud.

The laws of the Mosaic code concerning marriage have pre-eminently a negative character, prohibiting that by which the purity and sacredness of the conjugal life might be disturbed and defiled. They are very explicit, especially in regard to prohibited marriages. Adultery and incestuous connections, within certain degrees, are treated as capital crimes. Concerning the mutual rights and duties of husband and wife and concerning divorce only a few positive provisions are made and some occasional hints are given. No fixed forms of concluding marriage are expressly mentioned. Whatever the law omitted in this respect was probably left to the customs and usages which had been established prior to the Mosaic legislation.

The marital law of the Talmud, ([1]) which developed

([1]) The treatises of the Talmud almost exclusively devoted to the laws on Marriage and Divorce are the following: KIDDUSHIN (on betrothment); KETHUBOTH (on dower and marriage settlements); YEBAMOTH (on levirate and prohibited marriages); SOTA (on the woman suspected of adultery); GITTIN (on divorce). Besides, these laws are occasionally discussed also in other parts of the Talmud.

during the period of the second Temple and the first centuries after its destruction, is an interpretation and enlargement of the Mosaic laws. The enlargement consists partly in extended provisions, made by analogy and deduction from the Biblical law, partly in the embodiment of those norms and usages which had been handed down by tradition from time immemorial, and which now became a part of the law; partly, in new regulations enacted by the SOPHERIM (the Scribes) and later religious and civil authorities, according to the exigencies of the changed times and circumstances. The forms of concluding and dissolving marriage, as well as the marital rights and duties, are minutely defined and regulated, and, besides, innumerable casuistical questions concerning this relation are particularly treated of in the Talmudic Law. Several of these regulations, however, underwent some modifications by the decisions of the GAONIM, who, after the close of the Talmud, flourished as the heads of the Babylonian Academies to the eleventh century.

While the law in general is treated of in the Talmud in discussions and controversies, several authorities in the Middle Ages furnished codified abstracts thereof, for practical use. The most important of these systematized codes, in which due regard is paid, also, to the decisions of the Gaonim and later authorities, are: 1, YAD HACHEZAKA of Maimonides, in the twelfth century, and 2, the SHULCHAN ARUCH of R. Joseph Karo, sixteenth century. Of the fourteen books into which the former is divided, the fourth, termed Sepher Nashim (comprising Hilchoth Ishuth, H. Gerushin, H. Yibbum uchalitza, H. Naarah Bethula and H. Sota), is devoted to the laws concerning the matrimonial relation; while the Shulchan Aruch treats of the same subject in the third part, termed EBEN HA-EZER, which is divided into 178 chapters. This latter code, together with the annotations by R. Moses Issrels, and other casuists, obtained general authority in Judaism, and down to our own time all questions concerning marriage and divorce have been decided according to its rules and regulations.

MODERN MODIFICATIONS.

§ 4.

Strict adherence to the *dicta* of this rabbinical code, was possible only as long as the Jews in the different countries of the Old World occupied an exceptional position and were subject to a distinct judicature, regulated to a certain extent by their own laws, especially in all matters touching marriage, divorce, and hereditary succession. In modern times it is different. Since the Jews, in most of the European countries, have in all civil affairs been placed on the same footing before the law with their fellow-citizens, the Jewish courts have been abolished. The rabbi is no longer, as formerly, at the same time the civil judge: he is now only the spiritual guide and adviser of his congregation. With the abolishment of the Jewish jurisdiction, that part of the rabbinical code which regulates the property and the mutual rights of husband and wife fell entirely into disuse. In this respect, as in all other purely civil affairs, the Jews in our time willingly submit to the regulations of the laws of that country whose citizens they are, according to the Talmudic maxim: "Dina d'malchutha dina"—The law of the country is the binding law. Also, many provisions of the rabbinical code, especially those concerning the dissolution of marriage, had necessarily to be modified in order to make them conform to the requirements of the laws of the different countries. Modern Jews, moreover, find several rules and formalities of the ancient marriage law to be obsolete and impracticable in our days. The necessity of revising the rabbinical code of marriage laws according to the changed views and circumstances of our time, has, during the last fifty years, been elaborately discussed by prominent German rabbis in Jewish periodicals, as well as in separate pamphlets. (¹)

Subsequently, several rabbinical conferences and synods, especially the conference of 1844, held in Braunschweig, Germany; the first Israelitish Synod, held in Leipzig in 1869, and the second, held in 1871 in Augsburg; and also the conference of American rabbis, held in 1869 in Philadelphia, discussed the subject and passed resolutions by which some of the objectionable provisions of the rabbinical code were declared abrogated and others were more or less modified. References to these resolutions will be made in the following chapters at the proper place.

---

(1) See · GEIGER, "Die Stellung des weiblichen Geschlechts im Judenthum unserer Zeit." Wissenschaftliche Zeitschrift fuer jued. Theologie III. 1-14.

HOLDHEIM, Autonomie der Rabbinen und Princip der jued. Ehe.

HOLDHEIM, Vorschlaege zu einer zeitgemaessen Reform der juedischen Ehegesetze. Schwerin, 1843.

See, also: GUTMANN's article on Levirate Marriage in Geiger's *Wissenschaftl. Zeitschrift IV.*, and in Stein's *Volkslehrer IV.*, and his and B. WECHSLER's articles on the formalities of the act of divorce in the latter periodical IX.

It must, however, be stated that the authority of these conferences is not generally acknowledged. Their resolutions are accepted only by the followers of the principles of modern Judaism, while our conservative co-religionists regard all the norms of the rabbinical code as ever binding and unchangeable.

CHAPTER III.

LEGAL VIEW OF MARRIAGE.

§ 5.

IN modern law writings, generally, marriage is denominated a CONTRACT—a contract by which man and woman reciprocally engage to live with each other during their joint lives, and to discharge toward each other the duties imposed by law on the relation of husband and wife. "Our law," says Blackstone,[1] "considers marriage in no other light than as a civil contract." It differs, however, from other contracts in this—that it can not be rescinded by either party or both at pleasure, though that effect is brought about in either way by certain kinds of misconduct. Taking marriage in this civil light, the common law treats adultery as an immoral act, indeed, which offers valid grounds for a divorce, but yet not, in itself, an indictable crime; it regards it rather as misconduct, a private injury, which may be condoned by the offended party.

The Roman Catholic Church holds marriage to be a sacrament, and, as such, indissoluble.

Between these two extreme views stands that of the Jewish law. The act of concluding marriage is there

---

[1] Comm. I. 432.

certainly also considered as a contract, which requires the consent of both parties and the performance of certain formalities, similar to other contracts, and which, under certain circumstances, can be dissolved. But, inasmuch as marriage concerns a relation which is based on morality and implies the most sacred duties, it is more than a mere civil contract. In such a contract, the mutual duties and rights emanate from the optional agreement of the contracting parties, while those who enter upon the state of married life must submit to the reciprocal duties which have been imposed by religion and morality. (¹)

---

(1) Compare Dr. Z. Frankel's Grundlinien des mosaisch-talmudischen Eherechtes, page 4: "Das mos.-talm. Eherecht kann zwar nicht umhin, das *Eingehen* der Ehe als Vertrag zu betrachten; das Schliessen der Ehe beruht auf der freien Willenserklaerung; fehlt von einer Seite der Consent, so ist die Ehe unguelig; die *eingegangene* Ehe aber, die Ehe, sobald sie sich als Solche setzt, rueckt aus dem Gebiete des Vertrages in die hoehere, das Ganze des Menschen umspannende Sphaere der Sittlichkeit, vor der Willkuehr und Einzelwille aufgeht."

Similar to this view is that of Kalisch's Commentary on Leviticus, II. volume, p 247: "The conclusion of a marriage partook, indeed, of the character of a contract, since it required the full agreement of both parties; but as soon as the marriage was concluded it was withdrawn from the arbitrary will of both husband and wife, and was removed to the higher sphere of duty and conscience." Compare, also, Leopold Loew's "Eherechtliche Studien," in Ben Chananja, vol. iii., p. 211.

Some very distinguished English and American writers on the Marriage Law almost coincide with the Jewish conception of the marriage contract, stated above, as may be seen from the following definition in Bishop's Commentaries on the Law of Marriage and Divorce, I. § 3: "While the contract is merely an executory agreement to marry, it differs not essentially from other executory civil contracts. * * * But when the contract is executed in what the law regards as a valid marriage, its nature as a contract is merged in the higher nature of the *status*. And, though the new relation—that is, the *status*—retains some similitude reminding us of its origin, the contract does in truth no longer exist, but the parties are governed by the law of husband and wife. In other words, when the parties agreed to be married, they undertook only to assume the marital *status*; and, on its assumption, the agreement, being fully performed according to its terms, bound them no longer."

Adultery is not merely infidelity toward the conjugal partner, but a violation of a divine order, a crime which can not be condoned by the offended party; it invalidates the very foundation of that marriage, so as to make its continuation absolutely impossible. (¹)

The higher nature of the marriage contract is also indicated by the peculiar and significant term used in the Jewish Law for this contract. It is called *Kiddushin*—"consecration," from the Hebrew word *kaddesh*—to consecrate, to set apart as holy and inviolable. The idea connected with this term is, however, quite different from that of *sacrament* in the Catholic Church, as will be seen from the following definition given by the rabbis: "The act of contracting marriage is termed *Kiddushin*, since by this act the wife is set apart for her husband, and rendered inviolable and inapproachable in respect to any other man. (²)

(¹) Under Jewish jurisdiction the husband was compelled by court to divorce his wife who had been found guilty of adultery. See Eben Ha-Ezer, chapter CXV. 7, 8.

(²) Talmud Kiddushin, 2b.—Another rabbinical term for the marriage contract is *Arusin*, or *Erusin* (אירוסין), from the Biblical word *aras* (ארש), to betroth, to espouse, to bind in marriage. The state of matrimony, or the legal relation of marriage, is termed in the Rabbinical Law *Ishuth*, from the Hebrew *Ish*—the husband. The Biblical language, not having many terms for abstract legal ideas, expresses the relation of marriage more concretely by *husband* and *wife*, in connection with verbs or adjective pronouns, as, having a husband, taking a wife, his wife, her husband.

CHAPTER IV.

MONOGAMY AND POLYGAMY.

a. BIBLICAL AND TALMUDICAL PERIOD.

§ 6.

ACCORDING to the ideal of marriage as presented in the history of creation and in all ethical parts of Scripture, marriage is the union of one man with only ONE woman. Polygamy, however, actually prevailed among almost all oriental nations of antiquity, where it seems to have been necessitated by climatic and other circumstances.(¹) The Mosaic Law obviously regarded polygamy as an evil which, like slavery, revenge for bloodshed, and other evils, under the existing circumstances, could not at once be eradicated and in some way was preferable to the greater evil of concubinage. The law, therefore, endured polygamy under some restrictions, without, however, expressly sanctioning it. On the one hand, it provides for cases where a man is married to more than one wife (Exod. xxi. 9; Lev. xviii. 18; Deut. xxi. 15–17), while on the other hand, many of its provisions presuppose monogamy as the rule (Deut. xx. 7; xxiv. 5; xxv. 5–11). Several of its provisions are evidently calculated

---

(1) Compare Montesquieu's Esprit des Lois, XVI. 2–7.

to render polygamy very inconvenient and in this way to prepare for its final abolishment. Such a tendency is evident, especially, in the prohibition as to the neglect of conjugal duties toward the one wife on account of another. (Ex. xxi. 9.)

Moses himself lived in monogamy : so did Aaron, the high priest and his successors. The passage (Lev. xxi. 13)—"And he shall take a (one) wife in her virginity" (1)—is generally regarded as a restriction upon the high priest, that he shall not be married to more than one wife at the same time. The prophets are nowhere mentioned as having lived in polygamy. The kings, however, did so generally, though they were expressly forbidden by the law to multiply wives greatly. Among common people, monogamy seems to have been the rule, and polygamy the exception. Even wealthy men like Nabal and the Sunnamite woman's husband were monogamists. The custom of taking another wife in addition to the first was probably confined to cases where the former marriage was childless, or where a married man had, according to the law, taken his childless brother's widow.

The Talmudic period did not differ much in this respect from the Biblical. (2) None of the public teachers during,

---

(1) Talm. Yebamoth 59a· אשה אחת ולא שתים; see, also, Maimonides, Issure Biah XVII. 13.

(2) That polygamy, though permitted by the law, was disapproved by the popular morals and regarded as incompatible with domestic peace and happiness, is, among others, evident from a remarkable passage in the Aramaic paraphrase of the book of Ruth. In this paraphrase (Targum), which originated during the Talmudic period, the kinsman of Elimelech being requested by Boaz to marry Ruth and redeem her deceased husband's inheritance, answers the following (iv. 6): "I can not marry her, *for I am already married, and am not*

this period is mentioned as having been married to more than one wife at a time. Still, polygamy existed legally, and the provisions of the Talmudic law frequently refer to cases where one man contracts marriage with more than one wife. Several rabbinical enactments, however, must have proved efficient obstructions to polygamy; for instance, the provision that no man could contract marriage without securing to his wife a dowry for the case of his death or divorce. According to the opinion of some authorities, the first wife had a right to claim a bill of divorce in case her husband took another wife without her consent. (¹)

b. RABBINICAL INTERDICTION OF POLYGAMY.

§ 7.

An express prohibition of polygamy was not pronounced until the convening of the Rabbinical Synod at Worms, under the celebrated Rabbi Gershom ben Juda, in the beginning of the eleventh century. (²) Though this prohibition was originally made for the Jews living in Germany and Northern France, it was successively adopted in all European countries. Nevertheless, the Jewish Marriage Code retained many provisions which originated at a time when polygamy was still legally in existence.

The consequences of retaining such antiquated pro-

---

allowed to marry another wife in addition to her. This would mar the peace and happiness of my house. But thou mayest marry her, as thou art not yet married."

(¹) Yebamoth 65a. כל הנושא אשה על אשתו יוציא ויתן כתובה.

(²) See Eben Ha-Ezer I. 10.

visions will be seen in the following instance: According to modern laws, strictly based on the principle of monogamy, a prior subsisting marriage of EITHER OF THE PARTIES renders the second marriage absolutely null and void. But according to the rabbinical code a distinction is made between the case of the man and that of the woman. If marriage is contracted with a married woman whose husband is still living, that marriage is certainly null and void from the beginning; (¹) but if a man whose prior marriage is still subsisting contracts a second marriage, that second marriage is regarded valid in so far as it requires a formal bill of divorce for its dissolution. (²)

In view of the great inconveniences into which the deceived woman under certain circumstances is brought in such a case, the Philadelphia Rabbinical Conference unanimously passed the following resolution:

"Polygamy contradicts the idea of marriage. The marriage of a married man to a second woman can, therefore, neither take place nor claim religious validity, just as little as the marriage of a married woman to another man, but like this it is null and void from the beginning." (³)

c. CIRCUMSTANCES INFLUENCING THE PREVALENCE OF MONOGAMY.

§ 8.

The prevalence of monogamy among the civilized nations is not to be exclusively ascribed to the influence of

---

(¹) See Eben Ha-Ezer XVII. 1.
(²) See Eben Ha-Ezer I. 10, gloss. 3; also, DARKE MOSHE, note 1 to Tur E. H., chapter xliv.
(³) Protokolle, p. 26.

Christianity, as the New Testament does not expressly condemn polygamy, but only ordains that the bishop or presbyter shall have but one wife. (¹) It was rather a consequence of the circumstance that monogamy was more congenial to the climate and customs of European nations, as it primitively prevailed among Greeks and Romans, as well as among the ancient Germans; (²) though, on the other hand, the purity of marriage was greatly polluted among those nations by the custom of concubinage. This circumstance, in connection with the ethical teachings of the Bible, finally effected that monogamy was declared by the laws of Justinian as the exclusive form of marriage, (³) and this law was subsequently adopted into the codes of all civilized nations, so that bigamy or polygamy are punished as a crime.

---

(1) I. Timothy, iii. 2.

(2) Tacit. de mor. Germ., c. 18: "Prope soli barbarorum singulis uxoribus contenti sunt;" see, also, Cæsar De bello Gallico I., c. 38.

(3) Inst. I, 10, 6: "Duas uxores eodem tempore habere non licet."

PROHIBITED MARRIAGES.

The marriages prohibited in the Jewish law may be divided into the following classes:

A. Prohibitions on account of Consanguinity and Affinity.

B. Prohibitions in consideration of Chastity.

C. Prohibitions for religious and other reasons.

CHAPTER V.

A. CONSANGUINITY AND AFFINITY.

§ 9.

Regarding consanguinity and affinity, difference is made between those prohibited in the Mosaic Law, which are termed עריות, incestuous connections, and those prohibited by the Sopherim (Scribes), which are denominated שניות, secondary ordinances concerning incestuous connections. A marriage within the former degrees is absolutely null and void from the beginning, so that no divorce is required for its dissolution, while a consummated marriage within the second class of prohibited degrees is voidable, that is, merely subject to dissolution, and hence requires a formal act, a bill of divorce. (¹)

a. BIBLICAL DEGREES.

§ 10.

The Biblical degrees of consanguinity and affinity are contained in Leviticus, chap. xviii., and repeated also in Lev. xx. 11–21, where certain punishments are appointed for particular kinds of incestuous connections. Besides, some of these degrees are mentioned also in Deut. xxiii. 3, and xxvii. 20, 22, 23, in connection with other execrable crimes.

The first-mentioned chapter is introduced by the words: "Like the doings of the land of Egypt wherein you dwelt, shall you not do, and like the doings of the land of Canaan, whither I bring you, shall you not do. * * * *

(¹) הא הפסו בהן קידושין, Talm. Kiddushin, p. 67*b*; Maim. Ishuth IV. 12, 14; Eben Ha-Ezer XV. 1; XLIV. 6, 7.

By the common law of England, marriages within the prohibited degrees of consanguinity and affinity are voidable, not void. But by statute of the year 1835 it was provided that all marriages thereafter solemnized, within the prohibited degrees either of consanguinity or affinity, should be void. (Bishop's Marr. and Div., I., § 119.) In most of the American States such marriages are by statute void, in some voidable only. (*Ibid.*, § 320.) The difference between void and voidable, as set forth by Bishop (§ 105), is the following: "A marriage is said to be void when it is good for no legal purpose, and its invalidity may be maintained in any proceeding, in any court, between any parties, whether in the lifetime or after the death of the supposed husband and wife, and whether the question arises directly or collaterally. A marriage is said to be voidable, when the imperfection can be inquired into only on a proceeding conducted for the purpose of setting it aside, during the lifetime of both the husband and wife. Until set aside, it is practically valid; when set aside, it is rendered void from the beginning."

None of you shall approach to any that is near of kin to him, to uncover their nakedness. I am the Lord" (verses 2–6.)

After enumerating the cases of prohibited connections, the chapter concludes with the warning: "Do not defile yourselves with any of these things, for by all this the nations are defiled which I cast out before you. * * * I am the Lord your God." (verses 24–30.)

This exhortation at the beginning and the impressive warning at the conclusion of the chapter sufficiently characterize the prohibitions enumerated as not ceremonial ordinances nor political statutes, but divine laws based on morality, and, like all moral precepts, binding upon all nations and intended to be unalterable in all times.

The order in which the prohibited alliances are enumerated in the Mosaic Law (Lev. xviii.) is the following:

1. Mother. (v. 7.)
2. Stepmother. (v. 8.)
3. Sister and half-sister. (vs. 9 and 11.)
4. Granddaughter (son's or daughter's daughter). (v. 10.)
5. Father's sister. (v. 12.)
6. Mother's sister. (v. 13.)
7. Father's brother's wife. (v. 14.)
8. Son's wife. (v. 15.)
9. Brother's wife (except in the case of levirate). (v. 16.)
10. Wife's mother. (v. 17.)
11. Wife's daughter (stepdaughter). (v. 17.)
12. Stepson's daughter. (v. 17.)
13. Stepdaughter's daughter. (v. 17.)

14. Wife's sister (during the life of the former). (v. 18.)

In this list DAUGHTER is not expressly mentioned, but she is *a fortiori* implied in the prohibition of granddaughter, stepdaughter and daughter-in-law.

The prohibitions of these degrees, which, on account of the name of the book in which they are set forth, are commonly termed the LEVITICAL DEGREES, are so evidently founded on moral considerations as to find a place in the code of every civilized nation of our time. (¹)

The Talmud finds these biblical prohibitions to be as manifestly resting on common sense and morality as the prohibitions of murder and theft. (²)

PHILO (de specialibus Legibus, p. 778), SAADJA (Emunoth ve-Deoth III.), MAIMONIDES (More Nebuchim iii. 49), and modern scholars assigned different reasons for these prohibitions. The most plausible of these reasons are, that the toleration of such connections between near relatives would impair the quiet and concord of families and endanger female chastity in the domestic circle. Hereto must, in regard to consanguinity, still be added the physiological reason of degeneration, as marriages between

---

(1) The English law, being in this respect mostly based on the Canonical law, adds to these Levitical Degrees several extensions, which partly go even beyond those made by the rabbis, as will be seen further on. The law of other Protestant countries, however, as the Prussian code, though in general adopting the prohibition of consanguinity and affinity, disregards the Levitical Degrees in this, that it neither interdicts alliances with the aunt nor with the brother's widow. See Preuss-Landrecht, Th. ii., Tit. 1, § 3.

(2) See Talmud Yoma, p. 67b. Maimonides seems to have had a different version of that passage, since he in his Sh'mone Perakim, chapter vi., maintains that the Talmud classifies the prohibited degrees among those positive laws which are not conceivable by human understanding.

persons closely allied in blood are apt to produce an offspring feeble in body and tending to insanity in mind. (¹)

b. TALMUDICAL EXTENSIONS.

§ 11.

By the authority of the Sopherim, the Talmudic law partly extended the Biblical prohibitions to the ascending and descending lines of whatever degree, partly went one degree above the Biblical, partly added a new homogeneous degree. (²)

(a) The first-mentioned extensions are in general of very slight practical consequence, on account of the great disparity of years between the parties. The extensions are made in the following cases:

---

(1) See Bishop's Marr. and Div., i., § 313.

(2) Talm. Yebamoth, p. 21: Maimonides Ishuth I. 6; Eben Ha-Ezer XV. The guiding principle of the rabbinical Law was to extend the prohibition to the whole line wherever the Mosaic law refers to lineal ascendants or descendants, and also, where a mistake might easily be made on account of a common appellation. Thus, MOTHER's mother's mother, and so upward, is forbidden, because the mother is interdicted in the Mosaic Law; while the extension to the FATHER's mother, though not mentioned in the Mosaic Law, was made because the appellation GRANDMOTHER is used without distinction for both the mother's and father's mother. It is hardly necessary to remark, that in making these extensions *ad infinitum* the rabbis had merely THEORETICAL consequences in view, just as the "Table of Kindred and Affinity" of the Anglican Church, interdicting thirty alliances to men, and the same number to women, opens with: "A man may not marry his—1, grandmother; 2, grandfather's wife; 3, wife's grandmother."

Of more practical purport are the extensions going only one degree above the Biblical prohibitions in the lateral lines. They are partly deduced from them by analogy, partly intended to be a preventive against transgressing the express interdictions of the Mosaic Law.

As the mother is forbidden, so is the grandmother and the great-grandmother, and so upward.

As the stepmother is forbidden, so is also the father's or mother's, or the paternal grandfather's stepmother, and so upward.

As the wife's mother is forbidden, so her grandmother, and so upward.

As the wife's daughter (stepdaughter) is forbidden, so her granddaughter, and so downward.

As the son's wife is forbidden, so the grandson's wife, and so downward.

As the granddaughter, so the son's or the daughter's granddaughter, and so downward.

(*b.*) Of the extensions going only one degree above the Biblical prohibitions in the LATERAL lines, we mention the following:

As the father's and mother's sisters are forbidden, so are the grandfather's and grandmother's sisters.

As the father's brother's wife is forbidden, so is also the paternal grandfather's brother's wife.

(*c.*) One new degree homogeneous to the Biblical was added in the following case: While the Mosaic Law expressly forbids only the FATHER's brother's wife, the Talmudic Law adds also the MOTHER's brother's wife, and besides, the father's uterine brother's wife.

According to the opinion of some authorities, it is against decency, though not against the law, for a man to marry the stepmother of his deceased wife. (¹)

(¹) Jerus. Talm. Yebamoth ii. 4; Eben Ha-Ezer XV. 24.—The Roman law prohibits such a marriage on the principle of *respectus parentelae*, since the widower must look upon his wife's stepmother as upon his own mother.

c. NOT OBJECTIONABLE DEGREES.

§ 12.

1. THE DECEASED WIFE'S SISTER. — In prohibiting a man's marrying his wife's sister, the law (Lev. xviii. 18) expressly adds the limitation, "in her LIFETIME." It is but a logical inference that, when the limitation is removed, the prohibition loses its force, and permission is implied to marry the sister of a DECEASED wife. This is the undisputed view of the Rabbinical Law. (¹)

2. UNCLE AND NIECE. — While the law explicitly forbids marriage between nephew and aunt (Lev. xviii. 12–14 and xx. 19, 20), it contains no prohibition for an uncle to marry his niece. The Rabbinical Law not only permitted, but even recommended marriage between uncle and niece. (²)

---

(1) Talm. Yebamoth 49a; Maim. Issure Biah ii. 7, 9; Eben Ha-Ezer XV. 27.—In most of the Protestant States of Europe, as also in every State in the Union, except Virginia, marriage with a sister of a deceased wife is lawful. In England, however, it is regarded unlawful and incestuous under the Levitical Law, and, strange enough, even a Jewish scholar of our time, Dr. M. Kalisch, in his Commentary on Leviticus (ii. 395), defends the English view by the spirit of the Levitical Law.—In most Catholic countries such marriages are formally prohibited, but dispensations are easily obtained.

(2) Talm. Yebamoth 62b; Maim. Issure Biah ii. 14; Eben Ha-Ezer ii. 6, gloss.—The permission in this case might seem inconsistent, as the degree of relationship between uncle and niece is the same as that between aunt and nephew. Modern scholars have tried to explain this in different ways. MICHAELIS, Mos. R., § 117, asserts that "Orientals regard the niece as a more distant relation than the aunt." EWALD, Antiquities of Israel, p. 197, says: "Connections between the uncle and the niece were allowed, manifestly, because here the respect due to the father or mother appeared to be less infringed." PHILIPPSON gives another reason, based on the principle which, according to his ingenious demonstration, underlies the Mosaic Law on prohibited degrees; see his Israelit. Bibel, second edition, i. p. 624. Others, again, hold that

3. Cousins.—The marriage between cousins is perfectly permitted by the Jewish Law. (¹)

4. Step-brothers and Sisters.—Perfectly permitted is also the marriage between persons who are step-brothers and step-sisters, from both sides, that is, between the children of a widower and of a widow who entered into matrimony. (²)

---

in prohibiting the marriage of nephew and aunt the law was principally guided by the consideration of the conflict between the marital authority which a husband is to maintain and that authority which an aunt ordinarily exercises over her nephew, while such a consideration entirely falls away in the case of an uncle marrying his niece.

The Canonical Law of the Roman Church, which greatly extended the Levitical Degrees, prohibits the marriage between uncle and niece. The English Law does the same, being to a great extent based on the Canonical Law. But in other Protestant States of Europe such marriages are allowed. In some of the States of this country, as in Ohio, Illinois, Michigan and Louisiana, they are unlawful by statute.

(1) Eben Ha-Ezer XV. 17.—In Ohio, marriages between first cousins are unlawful, but such marriages are here regarded as valid, if made in in a State where no such prohibition exists.

(2) Talm. Sota 43b; Eben Ha-Ezer XV. 11.—Although such persons can in no sense be called blood relatives, some of the Palestinian authorities were of the opinion that such an intermarriage ought to be forbidden on account of bad appearance. This opinion is, however, rejected.

TABLE OF PROHIBITED DEGREES.

BIBLICAL PROHIBITIONS | *TALMUDICAL EXTENSIONS.*

A. CONSANGUINITY.

a. IN THE ASCENDING LINE.

1. Mother. | Grandmother (paternal as well as maternal)

b. IN THE DESCENDING LINE

2. Daughter (implied in granddaughter).
3. Granddaughter (son's or daughter's daughter). | Son's or daughter's granddaughter.

c. COLLATERAL CONSANGUINITY.

4. Sister and half-sister (either born in wedlock or not)
5. Father's sister. | Grandfather's sister.
6. Mother's sister. | Grandmother's sister.

B. AFFINITY.

a. THROUGH ONE'S OWN MARRIAGE.

7. Wife's mother. | Wife's grandmother.
   | Wife's step-mother not strictly prohibited, but objectionable
8. Wife's daughter (step-daughter).
9. Wife's granddaughter.
10. Wife's sister (during the lifetime of the divorced wife).

b. THROUGH MARRIAGE OF NEAR BLOOD RELATION.

11. Father's wife (step-mother). | Father's or mother's stepmother.
12. Father's brother's wife. | Mother's brother's wife; father's uterine brother's wife.
13. Son's wife. | Grandson's or great-grandson's wife.
14. Brother's wife (except in the case of levirate).

CHAPTER VI.

B. PROHIBITIONS IN CONSIDERATION OF CHASTITY.

Besides the impediments of consanguinity and affinity, the Jewish Law contemplates several impediments which evidently are based on considerations of chastity.

I. THE DIVORCED WIFE.

§ 13.

According to the Mosaic Law, a man is not permitted to remarry his divorced wife who had married a second time and become a widow or been divorced from her second husband. (1)

Neither, according to the Rabbinical Law, is a man permitted to remarry his former wife whom he divorced on the express ground of her bad reputation or on account of her barrenness. (2)

II. THE ADULTERERS.

§ 14.

He who had committed or was under strong suspicion

---

(1) Deut. xxiv. 4; compare, also, Jeremiah iii. 1. According to Nachmanides, this law was intended to prevent the immoral practice of exchanging wives, which practice prevailed among ancient nations.

(2) Mishna Gittin IV. 7, 8; Maimonides Gerushin X. 12, 13; Eben Ha-Ezer X. 3.

of having committed adultery with another man's wife is not permitted to marry her in case she becomes divorced from her former husband or be left a widow. (¹)

III. SUSPICION.

§ 15.

Whoever assisted at a divorce as witness or agent is, according to the Rabbinical Law, not permitted to marry the divorced woman, if the circumstances justify the suspicion that his co-operation was prompted by the intention to marry her.

For a similar reason, he who testified to the death of an absent husband can not marry the widow of that husband. (²)

IV. MAMZER.

§ 16.

The word MAMZER, usually translated BASTARD, denotes, according to rabbinical interpretation, one born of incest or adultery. The Mosaic Law: "A *mamzer* shall not enter into the congregation of the Lord" (Deut. xxiii. 3), is explained to mean that neither persons born of incest or adultery nor any of their descendants, are permitted to marry Israelitish women, and that an Israelite is not

---

(¹) Talmud Sota 25; Yebamoth 24b; Maim. Sota ii. 12; Eben Ha-Ezer XI. 1.—Also by the Roman Law, which has been adopted in some of the United States, a person who had committed adultery, and for this cause was divorced, at the suit of the innocent party, could not afterward marry the partner of his or her guilt. See BOUVIER, Institutes, I., § 255. Similar provisions are also found in the Prussian "Landrecht," § 25, 28 sq., and in the Austrian Civil Code, § 67.

(²) Talm. Yebamoth 25a; Maim. Gerushin X. 14; Eben Ha-Ezer XII. 1, 2

permitted to marry a female *mamzer* or a woman descended from a *mamzer*. (¹)

A marriage between a *mamzer* and a female *mamzer* or between either of them and a proselyte is not objectionable. (²)

FOUNDLINGS and persons whose paternal descent is unknown are regarded in the Rabbinical Law as doubted *mamzers* and subject to the same restrictions as an undoubted *mamzer*. On account of their doubtful character, such persons are not even permitted to intermarry, but their intermarriage with proselytes is not objectionable. (³)

V. SPADONES.

§ 17.

Persons violently or artificially emasculated are, according to the rabbinical interpretation of Deut. xxiii. 2, disqualified from entering marriage with an Israelitish woman. (⁴)

Natural defects, in this respect, however, do not preclude the contract of a legal marriage. (⁵)

In regard to defects in consequence of disease there is a difference of opinion between the rabbinical authorities. (⁶)

(¹) Talm. Yebamoth 49a; Maim. Issure Biah XV. i.; Eben Ha-Ezer IV. 1, 13.

(²) Eben Ha-Ezer IV. 22, 24.

(³) Talm. Kiddushin 74a; Eben Ha-Ezer IV. 36.

(⁴) Talm. Yebamoth 70, 75; Eben Ha-Ezer V. 1-10.

(⁵) *Ibidem* and Maim. Iss. Biah XVI. 8. A similar distinction is made in the Roman Law, L. 39, § 1; D. de J. D. (23, 3): "Si spadoni mulier nupserit, distinguendum arbitror, castratus fuerit nec ne, ut in castrato dicas, dotem non esse; in eo qui castratus non est, quia est matrimonium, et dos, et dotis actio est."

(⁶) See Eben Ha-Ezer V. 10.

CHAPTER VII.

C. PROHIBITIONS ON ACCOUNT OF RELIGIOUS AND OTHER CONSIDERATIONS.

I. INTERMARRIAGE.

a. BIBLICAL AND TALMUDICAL GROUND.

§ 18.

The Mosaic Law prohibits intermarriage with certain Canaanitish nations, seven in number: "Thou shalt not make marriages with them, thy daughter thou shalt not give unto his son, and his daughter shalt thou not take unto thy son." As a motive for this prohibition is added: "For they will turn away thy son from following me, to serve other gods." (Deut. vii. 3, 4.)

Actuated by this motive, and at the same time, by the desire to preserve the purity of the Jewish race, Ezra and Nehemiah extended the Mosaic prohibition of intermarriage so as to include all the pagan nations of the country, and with great rigor compelled those who had entered such marriages to separate from their heathenish wives. (Ezra ix. 1, 2; x. 10, 11; Nehemiah x. 31; xiii. 23-25.)

In the spirit of Ezra's ordinance, later religious authorities in the time of the Maccabeans and in the time of the wars against the Romans, interdicted matrimonial connections between Israelites and Gentiles, (¹) and this prohibition is the established law of the Talmud and the Rabbinical Code. (²)

A difference of opinion exists only as to whether the prohibition of intermarriage with any of the other nations besides those seven expressly mentioned in the law (Deut. vii. 3) is to be regarded as Mosaic or only Rabbinical. (³)

After having embraced the Jewish religion, Gentiles are perfectly admitted to intermarriage. (⁴)

No special provision is made in the Rabbinical Law concerning intermarriage with Christians. These, though in other respects not regarded as heathens, (⁵) were actually included in the general prohibition of intermarriage with Gentiles. On the other hand, the Christian emperors and the Canonical Law strictly interdicted all marriages between Christians and Jews. (⁶)

(¹) Talm. Aboda Zara 31b.

(²) Maim. Issure Biah XII. 1; Eben Ha-Ezer XVI. 1.

(³) Talm. Kiddushin 68b. The first opinion is ascribed to R. SIMON BEN YOCHAI, and the second to the other rabbis. Maim. Iss. B. XII. i., decides, according to R. Simon, but R. MOSE OF COUCY, in *Smag Larin* CXII. and Tur Eb. Ha-Ezer XVI. decide differently.

(⁴) Maim. Iss., B. XII. 22, 25; Eben Ha-Ezer IV. 9, 10.

(⁵) Talm. Chulin 13b: גרים שבחוצה לארץ לאו ע"ז הן, "the Gentiles among whom we are living now are no heathens." See, also, Rabbi Isaac ben Shesheth's (fourteenth century) Responses, No. 119: הנוצרים נקראים גרים תושבים; compare, however, Maim. Maachaloth Assuroth XI. 7.

(⁶) Thus, the Emperor Constantius prohibited the intermarriage between Jews and Christians under penalty of death. The prohibition was renewed by the later emperors. See Cod. Theod. Liber III. Tit. VII Lex II.; Cod. Just. Liber I Tit. IX. Lex VII.

b. THE QUESTION OF INTERMARRIAGE IN MODERN TIMES.

§ 19.

In the year 1807 Napoleon I. convened a Jewish Synod (Sanhedrin) in the city of Paris, and among other questions to be answered was also that as to whether Jews were permitted to intermarry with Christians. The answer was: "The great Sanhedrin declares that marriage between Israelites and Christians, contracted according to the laws of the 'Code Civil,' are, from a civil standpoint, binding and valid, and, although such marriages can not be invested with the religious forms, they shall not entail any disciplinary punishment (anathema)." (¹)

This declaration obviously retains the Talmudic principle that a marriage between Jews and Gentiles can not be invested with the sanction of religion. It does not say that intermarriages between Jews and Christians are permitted, but only that such a marriage, if contracted according to the civil law, is civilly binding; which, however, was not at all the question to be answered by the Sanhedrin. The remission of the disciplinary punishment of *cherem* (anathema) was rather illusive, since this disciplinary punishment had at that time already entirely fallen into disuse in France.

The Rabbinical Conference held at Braunschweig, Germany, in the year 1844, although intending merely to indorse the declaration of the above-mentioned Sanhe-

---

(1) The original reads as follows. "Le grand Sanhédrin déclare, en outre, que les mariages entre israélites et chrétiens, contractés conformément aux lois du Code Civil, sont obligatoires et valables civilement, et que, bien qu'ils ne soient pas susceptibles d'être revêtus des formes religieuses, ils n'entraineront aucun anathème." Récueil des lois, etc., par A. E. Halphen, Paris, 1851, p. 25.

drin, really went far beyond that declaration by resolving "that the intermarriage of Jews and Christians, and, in general, the intermarriage of Jews with adherents of any of the monotheistic religions, is not forbidden, provided that the parents are permitted by the law of the State to bring up the offspring of such marriage in the Jewish faith." [1]

This decision of the Braunschweig Rabbinical Conference, which entirely abandoned the Talmudic standpoint, has been strongly criticized not only, as was to be expected, by rabbis belonging to the conservative school, but even by some of the most pronounced advocates of reformed Judaism. [2]

Even the author of that resolution, Rabbi Dr. Ludwig Philippson, has since greatly modified his views concerning this subject, as may be seen from the following quotation from one of his later works:

"Religion must pronounce against mixed marriages. It has been said that such marriages will contribute toward the promotion of tolerance and toward bringing the different religions nearer to each other. But, on the other hand, it must be conceded that they contribute as well toward the weakening of true religiousness and sincerity in matters of faith. It is certainly our duty to widen the sway of tolerance so that it may rule over all classes and individuals, however they may differ in regard to creed and religious life. But this duty is not done by merely leveling the religious ground in order to gain a little more space for the dominion of tolerance.

---

[1] Protokolle der Rabbinerversammlung in Braunschweig, p. 73.
One of the members of that conference made the motion to add. "And the rabbi is permitted to solemnize such marriages," but this motion was not carried.

[2] A motion made in the Augsburg Synod to indorse the resolution of the Braunschweig Conference was tabled. See Verhandlungen der Zweiten isr. Synode, pp. 109, 110.

"Therefore, little as any true friend of religion and humanity could wish that religion should stand between those who sincerely love and cling to each other, deeply as it must pain him to grieve such persons, still, from the standpoint of religion and of a sincere religious life, he can not but disapprove of mixed marriages." [1]

The position of modern Judaism, in general, regarding the question of intermarriage is similar to that taken by Protestantism or Roman Catholicism, both of which discountenance mixed marriages on purely religious grounds.

The principal reasons against such intermarriages are, that peace and harmony can not be expected to reign supreme in a marriage in which the parties belong to religions so widely diverging from each other in regard to certain dogmas. Experience, besides, demonstrates that it is only in the rarest cases of such mixed marriages that domestic life can be conducted and children brought up in the spirit of our religion. Judaism being the religion of the minority, as a matter of self-preservation is, therefore, also opposed to mixed marriages, which, if prevalent, would weaken its influence and endanger its very existence.

c. FURTHER OPINIONS ON THE SUBJECT OF INTERMARRIAGE.

§ 20.

Considering the great importance of the question of intermarriage, we shall, in addition to the above, quote here the official opinions of two celebrated banner-bearers

---

[1] Israelitische Religionslehre (Leipzig, 1865), vol. iii., p. 250.

of modern Judaism, the late rabbis of Berlin, Dr. GEIGER and Dr. AUB. Both of them belonged to the committee appointed by the first Jewish Synod held at Leipzig in 1869, to report, among other questions, on that concerning marriage between Jews and Christians.

GEIGER, after having demonstrated the difference between the moral standing of the Gentiles of ancient times and that of the Christians of our days, comes to the conclusion:

"The marriage between a Jew and a Christian, when concluded in a legal manner (by civil authorities only), is by no means without moral worth, and religion, even from its standpoint, can not deny the validity of such a marriage.

"It is, however, a different question which faces us when we ask whether mixed marriages ought to be favored and encouraged by religion itself. On the one hand, it appears that the fraternity of the human race, which religion so emphatically proclaims as its highest ideal and hope, will be promoted by intermarriages. But, on the other hand, it must be conceded that the divergence of spiritual life resulting from the difference of creed is apt to disturb conjugal peace and mar the sincere union of hearts. Besides this, the apprehension of a mutually detrimental influence in regard to the religious views of either party can not well be suppressed. Religion, then, especially that religion which is not the prevailing one, and which, because of being in the minority, is always at some disadvantage, can not be fairly blamed if she hesitates to lend a helping hand to further such marriages, if she prefers, under such circumstances, rather to make the entrance into her folds less difficult to the outside party than otherwise, in cases of proselyting, her duty would prompt her." [1]

Dr. AUB, in his report on the question before us, says:

---

[1] Referate ueber die der ersten isr. Synode zu Leipzig ueberreichten Antraege, pp. 187, 188.

"According to some Biblical and even some rabbinical utterances, the marriage between Jews and Christians might be declared as sanctioned. Such intermarriages already occurred as early as the Middle Ages, until interdicted by the church. The moral possibility of such a marriage is conceivable only when both parties to the marriage disregard all positive doctrines and laws of their respective creeds and simply adhere to a natural religion. But as long as either of them clings to the doctrines of his original creed—one observing the Day of Atonement and the other celebrating Good Friday in order to obtain remission of sins—the two are not one, not of one mind. Mixed marriages are, as a rule, far removed from the ideal of marriage. At all events, the desire to have such a marriage sanctioned by a clergyman can, from the nature of the case, not be a strong and sincere one. Either both parties are indifferent to the claims of religion, or at least one of them is so—why, then, ask the assistance of a minister? Or both still adhere to their respective faiths—how, then, can the one party be satisfied with the forms of the other's faith? In such instances a cordial address could as well be delivered by any layman. This will, at all events, satisfy the Jewish party, whose faith recognizes no ordained priests.

"The education of the children that may be born of such wedlock is likewise a strong consideration against mixed marriages.

"Wherever the State permits such mixed marriages, they are legally and morally binding when performed by the civil authorities. The religious form or the church blessing, which is only a ceremony, may and should be a matter of indifference to a bridal pair belonging to different faiths. In Judaism, which has no priests and no sacramental marriage, the express approbation of the rabbi is, in such cases, of no use. He can and will tacitly and willingly accept the validity of the mixed marriage actually concluded according to the civil law." [1]

The late Rev. Dr. D. EINHORN expressed himself still more emphatically concerning the question before us.

---

[1] Referate ueber die der ersten israel. Synodeueberreichten Antraege, p. 193.

In a controversy regarding mixed marriages he held that "such marriages are to be strictly prohibited even from the standpoint of Reformed Judaism," and he added: "To lend a hand to the sanctification of mixed marriage is, according to my firm conviction, to FURNISH A NAIL TO THE COFFIN OF THE SMALL JEWISH RACE, WITH ITS SUBLIME MISSION." (¹)

CONCLUSION.

§ 21.

In conclusion, the latest enunciation concerning this subject may find here a proper place. It is that of the Rev. Dr. I. M. WISE, in a public lecture on "Intermarriage." (²)

After having reviewed the historical side of the question, he continues:

"This question in regard to intermarriage was raised by Napoleon I., to the Sanhedrin, which he convoked, and was

---

(1) See the *Jewish Times*, Vol. I., Nos. 45 and 48.—For the sake of impartiality, we shall state here that a few radical rabbis in Germany advocated mixed marriages and did not hesitate to solemnize them in the name of religion. Of those rabbis especial mention may be made of the late Dr. S. HOLDHEIM, who tried to defend his views in a pamphlet entitled "Gemischte Ehen zwischen Juden und Christen." (Berlin, 1850.) Here in this country, a similar position on this question is taken by the Rev. Dr. S. HIRSCH, who defends the permittance of solemnizing intermarriages under certain conditions, though he freely admits that he would not recommend such mixed marriages, as in nine cases out of ten they prove failures. See his article on this subject in the *Jewish Times*, I., Nos. 27-36, and EINHORN's reply in the articles quoted above. See, also, the articles "Zur Mischehenfrage," in *Die Deborah* XXIV., Nos. 16-22, in which some of the American rabbis expressed their different views on both sides of the question.

(2) Published in the *American Israelite* of the 21st of December, 1883.

raised again and again in various rabbinical conferences, and the decisions given were always unsatisfactory in principle. Moses forbade intermarriage with certain heathens to prevent the falling back of children of Israel to heathenism. Proceeding upon this principle, the rabbis of old applied this law to all heathens in any place. But those modern Sanhedrin and conferences maintain the Islam is no heathenism, Christianity is no heathenism; and yet they negatived the question of intermarriage as mere matter of discipline and utility, that we few Israelites be not lost among the vast multitudes of Christians and Mohammedans. Evidently those gentlemen have taken very low ground, non-justifiable in law.

"They might have taken a much higher and more holding ground. The peace, happiness and prosperity of the family, and the performance of its sacred duties to God and man, is the higher ground which they might have taken to much better advantage. As long as the orthodox Christian looks upon the Jew as a damned and doomed soul, of less worth here and worthless hereafter, peace and good will, mutual respect, confidence and genuine affection can hardly be expected to sway a durable scepter in the family, the members of which look upon one another with such degrading and damaging prejudices. The offspring of such families are usually the worst sufferers, and the duties of the family, upon which are based the morals, ethics, the weal of society and the country, naturally remain unfulfilled, or but partially fulfilled. Mutual respect is the first condition in a family, which is not well possible in connection with such prejudices. Again, as long as desertions, abandonments and divorces, adultery and concubinage are of daily occurrence, also, in the best classes of society, the Jew and the Jewesses had better wait before they marry out of the pale till the morals of society be improved in that particular respect.

"But then it might be urged that there are thousands and tens of thousands of individuals in this country who profess no religion at all; hence they are free of those prejudices. Why should any rabbi refuse to solemnize in behalf of Judaism the marriage of such irreligious parties, whose parents happened to be Jewish on the one side and Christian on the other, if no existing law restrains him? And we have seen that no such law rightfully exists. To this might be replied: Because the parties are irreligious; or because such solemnization would be a mere mockery to persons who profess no religion; and no rabbi will abuse the authority vested in him to perform the task of a lower magistrate; no rabbi has a right to act the part of an ordinary stage actor—to go through a performance and pronounce formulas and benedictions to parties who believe in neither, and can not consider themselves benefited by either, as the next justice of the peace can declare them man and wife without any performance or benediction.

"If the rabbi believes, as he ought to, that matrimony is a sacred institution, sanctified by the law of the covenant, by the expressed will of the Maker of man, in whose name and by the authority of whose revealed law he unites the couple before him in the holy covenant of matrimony, and invokes upon them God's blessing; he will not make a comedian of himself to do and say all that for persons who do not believe a word about it. If any one does not believe in the Living God of Israel and the Sinaic revelation, he has no reason whatever to believe in the sanctity of the marriage compact as being instituted by the law of God, and consequently has no cause to be married by a rabbi, who acts by that authority only. This is certainly higher ground, which it might be difficult to controvert." [1]

2. LEVIRATE AND CHALITZA.

a. BIBLICAL AND TALMUDICAL PRECEPT.

§ 22.

The widow whose husband had died childless, leaving, however, a brother, is not permitted to marry a stranger, unless the surviving brother declares that he is not wil-

---

[1] The lecture concludes with the suggestion that the question of intermarriage shall be decided, in connection with the proselyte question, by a Jewish Synod.

ling to marry her, and submits to the prescribed formality termed *Chalitza*. (Deut. xxv. 4-13.)

From Genesis xxxviii. 8, where ANAN is called upon to marry his brother ER's widow, it is evident that already in the patriarchal period it was an established custom that in the case of a man having died without children his surviving brother was in duty bound to marry the widow. (¹) The Mosaic Code retained this custom, so that the general prohibition of marrying the brother's wife (Lev. xviii. 16) was set aside in case that brother had died without descendants, in which case it was regarded as a duty incumbent on one of the surviving brothers to marry the widow in order to retain the name and family property of the deceased. Such a marriage is termed YIBBUM, from the Hebrew *yabam*, "brother-in-law." It is also termed LEVIRATE, from the Latin *levir*, which has the same meaning as *yabam*. The purpose of the levirate marriage was obviously to avert the extinction of the name of him who died childless, "that his name be not put out of Israel." Besides, it stood in connection with the ancient agrarian law in Israel, which tended to retain all property intact within each tribe and family. The brother-in-law, in marrying the widow, became the sole heir of her deceased husband's estate, which otherwise would have to be divided among all his brothers, who in this case were the legal heirs. (²)

(¹) The same custom has been found to exist among various oriental nations, ancient and modern. See BENARY, De Hebraeorum Leviratu (Berlin, 1835), p. 31 *ss*, and REDSLOB, Die Levirats-Ehe, bei den Hebræern (Leipzig, 1836), p. 7; compare, also, T. E. ESPIN, in Speaker's Comment. on the Pentateuch, p. 888.

(²) The connection of the levirate with the agrarian law is also indi-

In retaining this ancient custom, the Mosaic Law modified the former strictness thereof by permitting escape from that obligation, which under certain circumstances might be onerous and even repugnant. The surviving brother could refuse to marry that widow, but had to submit to the ceremony of *Chalitza*, which was of a somewhat stigmatizing character. The ceremony described in Deut. xxv. 7–10, consisted in this, that after the surviving brother had declared before the court his unwillingness to marry the widow, she was directed to loose his shoe from off his foot, spitting before his face and saying: "So shall it be done unto that man that will not build up his brother's house." (¹)

This formality having been performed, the widow was at liberty to marry a stranger.

The law concerning the levirate marriage and the act of *Chalitza* is very minutely elaborated in the Talmud and in the Rabbinical Codes. (²)

A divergence of opinion is expressed in the Talmud, as well as among the post-Talmudic authorities, as to

---

cated in the Talmud Yebamoth, 17b: יבום בנחכה הלא רחמנא. It must also be stated here that, according to Talmudic interpretation (*ibid.* p. 24a), the provision of the levirate law "that the first-born which she beareth shall succeed to the name of the deceased brother" (Deut. xxv. 6) is not to be taken literally as if the first child born in that marriage was to be named after its deceased uncle, but rather figuratively that the name of the deceased shall remain on the inheritance which passes to the surviving brother who accepts the levirate.

(¹) The formality of loosing the shoe was probably a symbolic expression of taking from the unwilling brother all right over the wife and property of the deceased, while that of spitting before his face was intended to aggravate the disgrace conceived to attach to his conduct.

(²) Talm. Yebamoth; Maimon. H. Yibbum u-Chalitza; Eben Ha-Ezer, chapters 156–176.

whether *Yibbum* or *Chalitza* is to be preferred, that is, whether it is better for the surviving brother to fulfill the duty of levirate marriage or to submit to the punishment for non-fulfillment; because it was considered doubtful whether he who marries his brother's widow with other than the purest motives is not actually committing incest. (¹)

The levirate marriage having been found in many cases very onerous and, especially since the abolishment of polygamy, often impracticable and impossible, it fell more and more into general disuse, so that the ceremony of *Chalitza* took its place, by which the widow received the permission of marrying a stranger.

To prevent the brother-in-law from exacting conditions from the widow who wished to be liberated from the restriction to her new marriage, it became customary that at the wedding of a young couple, the brothers of the bridegroom were induced to sign a document (termed *Sh'tar Chalitza*) declaring that, if circumstances should require it, they will execute the ceremony of *Chalitza* without any claim of remuneration.

b. MODERN VIEWS AND RESOLUTIONS OF RABBINICAL CONFERENCES.

§ 23.

Modern Judaism, in general, strongly objects to the whole formality of *Chalitza*. The levirate marriage having been entirely abandoned, this ceremony, which is so decidedly contrary to modern customs and views, has

---

(1) Yebamoth 39b; Bechoroth 13a; Eben Ha-Ezer 165.

been found to be superfluous and meaningless. For, why should the surviving brother and the unfortunate widow go through a disgracing formality to establish the non-fulfillment of a marriage which they are no more permitted to enter? The question of abolishing the whole formality has been discussed in different essays ([1]) and in several rabbinical conferences. The Conference of American rabbis, held in Philadelphia (1869) unanimously passed the following resolution:

"The precept of levirate marriage, and eventually of *Chalitza*, has lost to us all meaning, import and binding force." ([2])

A resolution to the same effect was passed after an elaborate discussion, also, by the Jewish Synod held at Augsburg (1871). It reads as follows:

"The Biblical precept concerning the *Chalitza* has lost its importance, since the circumstances which occasioned the levirate marriage and the *Chalitza* no longer exist, and the idea underlying this whole precept has become foreign to our religious and social views.

"The non-performance of the *Chalitza* is no impediment to the widow's remarriage

"For the sake of liberty of conscience, however, no rabbi will refuse, on request of the parties, to conduct the act of *Chalitza* in a proper form." ([3])

---

[1] Of the numerous essays and articles written on this subject special mention may be made of those of Rabbi M. GUTMANN, in GEIGER's *Wissenschaftliche Zeitschrift fuer jued. Theologie*, vol. IV., pp. 61–87, and in STEIN's *Volkslehrer*, 1854, Nos. 53 and 57; 1855, No. 62. See, also, Rabbi ISAAC M. WISE's article in *The American Israelite*, 1855, Nos. 38 and 39, and GEIGER's article in *Juedische Zeitschrift*, 1862, p. 35 *sq.*

[2] Protokolle der Rabbiner-Conferenz gehalten zu Philadelphia, p. 39.

[3] Verhandlungen der zweiten israelitischen Synode zu Augsburg, pp. 138–155.

3. PROHIBITIONS ESPECIALLY FOR AARONITES.

§ 24.

There are, in addition, some religious impediments to marriage which affected only the PRIESTLY TRIBE — the descendants of Aaron.

According to Leviticus xxi. 6, 7, 14, the priests were to maintain a peculiarly high standard of legal purity in their family relations, because it was their office to offer sacrifices to the Lord. Hence a common priest was not permitted to marry a PROSTITUTE, a PROFANE (*i. e.*, one descended from the illegitimate marriage of a priest) nor a DIVORCED woman; the high-priest was, besides, not to marry a WIDOW.

Though the priestly office was abolished with the destruction of the temple, the Rabbinical Law retained those prohibitions concerning the descendants of the priestly tribe (Aaronites or Cohanim) and implied in those prohibitions, also, that of marrying a proselyte woman. ([1])

In modern times, however, these prohibitions concerning the Aaronites are not generally regarded, and the Rabbinical Conference held at Philadelphia (1869) unanimously adopted the following resolution:

"The priestly marriage laws, which are predicated upon the sanctity of the Aaronites, have lost all significance, and are no longer to be respected, since the destruction of the temple and the cessation of the old sacrificial worship destroyed the basis upon which the exclusive position of the Aaronite was established." ([2])

---

(1) Maim. Iss. B. XVII.; Eben Ha-Ezer VI.
(2) Protokolle der Rabbiner-Conferenz abgehalten zu Philadelphia, p. 27.

A motion to the same effect was offered by Dr. GEIGER at the Leipzig Synod. (¹) It was referred to a committee for report, but no action was taken.

At the second Synod in Augsburg the prohibition of an Aaronite's marrying a proselyte was indirectly removed by the following resolution, which, though having a general character, refers to this special case :

"WHEREAS, The ordinances of the Christian Church and the laws of modern States are, in regard to the prohibited degrees of affinity, almost still more rigorous than the Jewish Marital Law; and whereas, they regard marriage as a moral union, and consequently, at its conclusion, forbid everything which is in the least against strict morality;

"Therefore, the Jewish Synod declares :

"That the Talmudical Marriage Law in reference to proselytes of heathen origin does not apply to such persons as are converted to Judaism from Christianity." (²)

(¹) Verhandlungen der ersten isr. Synode zu Leipzig, 1869, p. 260.
(²) Verhandlungen der zweiten iuedischen Synode, p. 156.

CHAPTER VIII.

TEMPORARY IMPEDIMENTS.

THERE are still some impediments which exist for a limited time only, after which they cease of themselves.

I. PREVENTIVE AGAINST UNCERTAINTY OF PATERNITY.

§ 25.

A widow, within ninety days after her husband's death, and also a divorced woman, within the same period from the day of having received the document of divorce, are prohibited from contracting a new marriage. (¹)

The reason of this rabbinical prohibition is to prevent an uncertainty of paternity in regard to the first child born in the second marriage. The lapse of ninety days is, however, required even in such cases where the wife can not well be presumed to have been pregnant at the time of her husband's death or her divorce. (²)

(¹) Yebamoth, p. 41; Maim. H. Gerushin XI. 18; Eben Ha-Ezer XIII. 1.

(²) The ancient Roman Law prohibited a widow to remarry before the lapse of ten months. The reason was there partly the apprehension of *turbatio sanguinis*, partly the regard of the respect due to the memory of the deceased. The French Law coincides with the ancient Roman Law. The Prussian Law requires the lapse of a year for a widow.

II. PREGNANCY AND THE SUCKLING CHILD.

§ 26.

A widow or a divorced woman, being in a state of pregnancy, is not permitted to remarry until after her delivery.

If the widow or the divorced woman has a suckling child, she is not to marry before twenty-four months after that child's birth. (¹)

The prohibition in both cases was prompted by a regard for the child's welfare. In the second case, especially, the prohibition was predicated upon the opinion, generally prevalent in ancient times, that it is necessary for a new-born child to be nursed at the mother's breast for a period of at least twenty-four months, which period might become shortened by the mother's new marriage.

The views of modern times differ also in this respect from those of former days, and, as circumstances often make it desirable for the widow to remarry before the lapse of two years, the Jewish Synod of Augsburg modified the law by the following resolution:

"A widow having a child from her former marriage need not wait longer than one year with her new marriage. Where particular circumstances in the interest of the widow or of the

---

Here in this country there is, in general, no law to regulate the time during which a woman must remain a widow before she marries a second time. But decency requires that no marriage shall take place till at least the end of one year. See BOUVIER, Institutes I. 291, and Law Dictionary, article "Widowhood."

(¹) Yebamoth, p. 42; Maim. Gerushin XI. 25; Eben Ha-Ezer XIII. 3, 11.

child render the postponement of the new marriage inadvisable, it may take place even before that period." (¹)

III. MOURNING.

§ 27.

According to the ritual law, no marriage is to be entered upon within the first thirty days of mourning for the death of a near relative. (²)

A widower is not to remarry before the lapse of three festivals after the death of his wife. (³)

The reason assigned to the latter restriction is, that it was regarded improper for the husband to live with a second wife while his heart is still filled with the memory of another one.

Under some circumstances, however, this restriction could be dispensed with, especially when the widower has little children who need the care of a second mother. (⁴)

IV. OBSTRUCTIVE DAYS.

§ 28.

On Sabbath and festivals no marriage is to be contracted, as such an act falls under the category of legal transactions, which, in general, are not permitted to be performed on consecrated days. (⁵)

(¹) Verhandlungen der zweiten Synode, pp. 71–74.

(²) Yore Dea, chapter 392, § 1.

(³) *Ibid.*; § 2.

(⁴) *Ibid.*, gloss.

(⁵) Talm. Betza, pp. 36, 37; Eben Ha-Ezer LXIV. 5; compare, also, Orach Chayim, chapter 339, § 4 and chapter 524, § 1.

The marriage contract, however, although performed on such days, is perfectly valid, if good in other respects. (¹)

In former times it was also customary not to celebrate marriages on certain days commemorating great national calamities in our history, especially during the days between the first and the ninth of the month of *Ab*, commemorating the destruction of the Temple. (²)

Some over-zealous authorities extended the time, making it from the 17th day of *Tamuz* to the Ninth of *Ab*. (³) For some unknown reasons, also, the days between *Pasach* and *Shabuoth*, with the exception of some single days, were added. (⁴) A popular superstition, consequently, looked upon those days as ominous for marriage; hence the custom of abstaining from celebrating marriage on such days is still kept up by many, though those days have otherwise ceased to be a time of mourning. (⁵)

(¹) Orach Chayim, *ibid.*; see R. Mos. Isserles' gloss to that paragraph.

(²) Orach Chayim, chapter 591, § 2.

(³) See R. Mos. Isserles' gloss to that paragraph.

(⁴) Orach Chayim, chapter 493.

(⁵) Rabbi Dr. Landsberger, in an elaborate and very interesting article in Geiger's *Juedische Zeitschrift fuer Wissenschaft und Leben* VII. pp. 81–96, proves the custom of abstaining from celebrating marriage between *Pasach* and *Shabuoth*, to be of heathen origin, as also among the ancient Romans the popular superstition prevailed that nuptials during the month of May portended ill luck to the young couple. Compare Ovid. Fast., lib. V. 487–490. From the Romans that superstition was transplanted to France, where it still prevailed in the seventeenth century. (Bayle *Pensees diverses*, § 100.) Walter Scott, in his third letter on Demonology and Witchcraft, p. 104, reports that he found the superstition also in Scotland.

The Jewish Synod of Augsburg, on motion, passed the following declaration concerning this unwarranted restriction:

"The custom of abstaining from performing the marriage ceremonies on certain days regarded as ominous, especially in the time between *Pasach* and *Shabuoth*, besides within the three weeks preceding the Ninth of *Ab*, with the exception of the three weeks in which *Tisha b'Ab* falls, is entirely without foundation; it contributes toward promoting superstition, and corresponds with no religious sentiment. The Synod, therefore, regards this restriction as abolished." [1]

---

[1] Verhandlungen, etc., pp. 76-79.

CHAPTER IX.

QUALIFICATIONS TO CONTRACT MARRIAGE.

THERE are certain requirements in the contracting parties which are so essential that their non-fulfillment, under certain circumstances, would invalidate the marriage, though formally concluded. These requirements are:

1. Consent of the parties.
2. Mental capacity.
3. The legal age.

I. CONSENT.

a. MUTUAL CONSENT.

§ 29.

The contract of marriage, like every other contract, requires the mutual consent of the parties. Without such a consent the marriage is void, though the prescribed forms have been complied with. [1]

A consent obtained by FORCE is no consent. Some authorities, however, make a difference between these two cases, viz., where the FEMALE or the MALE party had been forced to the marriage contract. In the former case the marriage is void; in the second it is regarded

---

[1] Maim. H. Ishuth IV. 1; Eben Ha-Ezer, XLII. 1.

as valid. The reason assigned for this distinction is the circumstance that, according to the ancient law, a wife could not divorce her husband, while he could divorce her even against her will. Hence, if he was not willing to accept the marriage forced upon him, he still had it in his power to free himself by a bill of divorce. (¹)

Since, however, in later times, by the authority of Rabbi GERSHOM (eleventh century), the rule was established that no man must divorce his wife against her will, both cases ought to be treated alike, and the marriage should be void, whoever may have been the forced party. (²)

b. CONDITIONAL CONSENT.

§ 30.

If the consent was given under certain conditions on either side of the parties, the validity of the marriage depends upon the strict fulfillment of those conditions. Such conditions must, however, be distinctly and precisely formulated according to certain rules of the Talmudic Law; otherwise they are without effect and have no influence upon the validity of the marriage contract. (³)

To understand the rabbinical provisions regarding conditional consent, it must be borne in mind that anciently, as will be seen in a following chapter, a period of one

---

(¹) See Maggid Mishne to Ishuth IV. 1.

(²) Compare Ture Zahab to Eben Ha-Ezer XLII. 1.

(³) The particulars concerning the form and nature of such conditions are found in Maim. Ishuth VI.; Eben Ha-Ezer XXXVIII.

month to a whole year usually intervened between the act of contracting marriage (termed *Kiddushin*) and the nuptials (termed *Nissu-in*). It then sometimes occurred that the consent to a contract of marriage was given on certain conditions, which, if not fulfilled, eventually vacated the contract. But the consummation of such a conditional contract by the nuptials, or by cohabitation, was regarded as a silent annulment of the conditions, so that their non-fulfillment did not affect the validity of the marriage. ([1])

It is hardly necessary to be stated that in our time, where the act of contracting marriage is combined with the nuptials on the wedding day, the consent of the parties to marriage must be ABSOLUTE, WITHOUT ANY CONDITIONS WHATEVER.

([1]) See Tal. Kethuboth 74a; Maim. Ishuth VII. 23; E. H. XXXVII. 35.—A certain analogy to this Rabbinical Law is found in modern law writing in reference to CONDITIONAL PROMISE OF FUTURE MARRIAGE, followed by cohabitation, and also in regard to MARRIAGES PROCURED BY FRAUD and duress. We quote the following: "If (in a conditional promise of future marriage) the condition is of a nature not to be purified until after the copula is had, the law will not found on the transaction a marriage; but, if the condition could be purified before, or at the time, the law will presume it was so purified, and will infer a present mutual consent. An illustration of the latter case is: If a man has agreed to marry a woman when he can do so with comfort, or when she finds caution that is free from debt, or worth a sum of money named, the condition, in its nature, may at any time be purified, and, if copula follows such a promise, the law will hold the parties to be married." Bishop, Mar. and Div. (fourth ed.), I. 263. Regarding a marriage procured by FRAUD, the same authority says (p. 218): "In fraudulent marriages, cohabitation, with knowledge of the fraud, will bar the right to have the marriage set aside. * * * We may observe that the fact of the marriage not having been consummated has in many instances powerfully influenced the court in favor of setting it aside."

C. ERROR AND FALSE REPRESENTATION.

§ 31.

Error in respect to the qualities of one of the contracting parties, as his fortune, rank, character and circumstances, does not render the marriage void, unless the consent had been given on the express condition that the representation made be verified. (¹)

Whether error respecting physical imperfections affects the validity of the marriage contract, is a doubtful question. Even if their non-existence had been stipulated, only certain imperfections, generally regarded as such, vitiate the contract. (²)

d. THE CONSENT OF PARENTS.

§ 32.

The consent of parents is no legal requirement when the parties to the marriage are of age. (³) In consequence of the high respect and veneration, however, in which father and mother have ever been held among

---

(¹) Maim. H. Ishuth VIII. 1, 6; E. H. XXXVIII. 24.—We may observe that an error in regard to the IDENTITY OF PERSON, as, if one person be substituted for another, will invalidate the marriage according to the Jewish Law, as well as it does according to the modern laws.

(²) Maim. Ishuth VII.; Eben Ha-Ezer XXXIX.

(³) Maim. Ishuth III. 12; Yore Dea, ch. 240, 25 gloss.—Also according to modern laws in general, the consent of parents is not required in order to give validity to a marriage. In some States there are provisions giving a right to the father to sue for a penalty the clergyman or magistrate who shall marry his minor child. 2 Kent's Com. 86: Bouvier Inst. I., No. 253. The last-mentioned law writer remarks, in this connection: "It is to be regretted that paternal authority is not more respected, for whenever that is disregarded other duties are neglected."

Israelites, the cases of contracting marriage without the parents' consent fortunately belong to the rarest exceptions.

2. *MENTAL CAPACITY.*

a. IDIOCY AND LUNACY.

§ 33.

Since consent is absolutely requisite to the marriage contract, neither idiots nor lunatics are capable of contracting a valid marriage. (1)

The marriage of a person subject to temporary insanity is, however, not void if contracted in his lucid intervals. (2)

Although it is very improper to enter upon the sacred relations of matrimonial life in a state of intoxication, still the marriage would not be void if contracted in such a state, provided the intoxication had not reached the degree of unconsciousness. (3)

b. THE DEAF AND DUMB.

§ 34.

Persons deaf and dumb were in ancient times generally looked upon as a kind of idiot, hence considered legally incompetent to contract marriage. The Talmudic Law, however, conceded them the power of concluding such a contract by means of signs; but this

---

(1) Maim. H. Ishuth IV. 9; Eben Ha-Ezer XLIV. 2.
(2) See R. M. Isserles' gloss to the section of E. H. just quoted.
(3) Maim. *ibid.* § 18; E. H. *ibid.* § 3.

3. *LEGAL AGE.*

a. AT WHAT AGE MARRIAGE IS LAWFUL.

§ 35.

In the ethical teachings of the Talmud the age of eighteen years is fixed as the proper period of entering the state of married life. (²) Certain considerations, however, rendered it advisable to permit marriage to take place at a still earlier period. (³)

The legal age for contracting a valid marriage is, according to the Talmudical Law, the age of puberty, which, in general, is assumed to be the completed thirteenth year in males and the completed twelfth year in females. (⁴) A marriage contracted by minors under that age is void. (⁵)

(¹) Talmud Yebamoth, p. 112b; Maim. Ishuth IV. 9; E. H. XLIV. 1. The laws of modern States declare such persons competent to contract a valid marriage.—Some learned rabbis of our time are of the opinion that the provisions of the Talmudic Law in this respect can not apply to the deaf and dumb of our days, who are for the most part well educated in the institutions established for this purpose, where they become enabled to communicate their ideas in writing, as well as in audible words. See the articles on this subject by A. Hochmuth, Leopold Loew, M. Duschak and S. Back, in Ben Chananja I., p. 374 sq.; 465 sq.; II. p. 79 sq.

(2) Aboth V. 13.

(3) Talmud Yebamoth 62; Kiddushin 29.

(4) Tal. Nidda, p. 44; Maim. Ishuth II. 1, 10.

(5) Kidd. 50; Maim. Ishuth IV. 7; Eben Ha-Ezer XLIII. 1.
According to the common law of this country, no persons are capable of binding themselves in marriage until they have arrived at the age of consent, which is fixed at fourteen in males and twelve in females. This law was no doubt borrowed from the Roman Law, which established the periods of twelve and fourteen as the competent age of consent to render the marriage contract binding. Kent's Com. II. 78.

b. THE MINOR DAUGHTER.

§ 36.

An exception to this rule was made in former times in favor of a minor daughter. Her father could give her in marriage before her puberty, and this marriage was regarded perfectly valid.

Without the father's consent, however, the marriage of the minor is void. (¹)

If she be fatherless, her mother or brother could give her in marriage; but in this case the contract is voidable at the election of the infant at the time of her becoming of age. She could then either confirm the marriage, thereby making it afterward ever binding without any further ceremonies, or she could protest against it. Such a protest, termed *Me-un* (מיאן), rendered the marriage void, and set aside the necessity of a divorce. (²)

In order to understand the impulse toward the custom of contracting marriage in behalf of minor daughters, which prevailed in oriental antiquity, it must be borne in mind in what a pitiable state of forlornness an unmarried female was, in case of her father's death or poverty. Careful fathers, therefore, tried to insure their minor daughters against such consequences by contracting marriage in their behalf, while under their authority. Such contracted infant marriages were, as a rule, not actually consummated before the parties had reached the age of puberty.

Even as early as in the third century, one of the most

---

(1) Maim. Ishuth III. 11, 13; Eben Ha-Ezer XXXVII. 1, 4.
(2) Maim. Gerushin XI.; Eben Ha-Ezer CLV.

celebrated Talmudic authorities, ABBA AREKA, of Sura, raised an emphatic protest against the practice of such infant marriages, by declaring: "It is a moral wrong that a father should contract a marriage in behalf of his daughter before she has attained the age of consent." (¹)

In disregard of this warning, the custom of giving infant daughters in marriage came again into vogue even among the European Jews during their severe persecutions in the Middle Ages. This disregard is excused by some rabbis of that period by the following remarks:

"The persecutions increase daily; we are driven from one place to the other, finding nowhere a refuge. If to-day we are able to provide for our daughters, we live in the painful uncertainty as to how it will be to-morrow. Therefore, we must try to secure a protection for our young daughters by their early marriage." (²)

It must be stated here that such infant marriages have long since ceased among us with the circumstances that so urgently necessitated them. (³) In this,

---

(¹) Talm. Kiddushin, p. 41.

(²) Tosafoth to Kiddushin, p. 41; R. ISSERLES' gloss to Eben HaEzer XXXVII. 8.
Maimonides, living in Egypt, where the Jews suffered no persecutions, adheres to the injunction of ABBA AREKA, mentioned above. Ishuth III. 19. Compare FRANKEL's *Grundlinien*, p. 29.

(³) The practice of infant marriages during the Middle Ages was not confined to Jewish circles alone, but was found also among Christians in different countries. This may be seen from the following provisions of the Ecclesiastical Law quoted by BISHOP, Marriage and Divorce, I. § 146:

"If either party to a marriage is below seven, it is mere nullity. If both parties have arrived at seven, and either one of them is below his or her age of consent, or if both are, they may still contract an inchoate or imperfect marriage. This marriage they can not avoid or annul, until

as in other respects, the Jews willingly yield to the laws and customs of the civilized countries in which they live, as free and faithful citizens.

---

the party discarding it has reached the age of consent for such party, whether it be twelve or fourteen; and perhaps not until the other has also arrived at his or her age of consent."

THE FORM OF CONCLUDING MARRIAGE.

As the formalities of concluding marriage in our days differ, in some respects, from those in ancient times, we shall treat them here in separate chapters.

CHAPTER X.

THE FORM OF MARRIAGE IN ANCIENT TIMES.

§ 37.

In the Mosaic Law no fixed forms of concluding marriage are mentioned, though the distinction occasionally made between the betrothed and the married woman (Deut. xx. 7; xxii. 22–29) points to some kind of formality by which that different state was marked.

It was not till the time of the Second Jewish Commonwealth, when the Rabbinical Law developed on the basis of the Mosaic Code, that certain legal formalities were established for the act of concluding marriage. The act consisted of two distinct parts, intervened by the lapse of a certain time—the BETROTHMENT and the NUPTIALS.

A. BETROTHMENT.

a. ITS TERM AND NATURE.

§ 38.

A betrothment is termed, in Rabbinical Law, *Kiddushin*, or, also, *Arusin*. The former of these two terms refers especially to the act of betrothing, while the latter indicates the state of being betrothed. The betrothed parties are called respectively *Arus* and *Arusa*.

The meaning of a betrothment, according to the Rabbinical Law, differs essentially from the idea usually connected with that term in our day. In modern law, betrothment is defined to be "a contract between a man and woman, by which they agree that at a future time they will marry each other." Such a contract is of a purely civil nature. It may be dissolved by either party or both at pleasure. If broken by one of the parties without a just cause, the other party can, at the most, bring action for breach of promise and claim recovery of damage.

The nature of betrothment, according to the Rabbinical Law, is quite different. There, a betrothal is not a mere promise to marry, but it is the very initiation of marriage. The betrothed parties are in some respects regarded as married, though not yet entitled to the marital rights nor bound to fulfill any of the mutual duties of conjugal life, as long as the marriage was not consummated by the nuptials. The betrothment could be dissolved only through death or a formal bill of divorce. Faithlessness on the part of the betrothed female was treated as adultery. Without having been formally divorced, she could not enter a marriage contract with another person; if entered upon, it was void.

The betrothal was usually, though not necessarily, preceded by an ENGAGEMENT, more, in our sense of the word, as a preliminary agreement of the parties to become united in marriage at some future time. Such an engagement was termed *Shidduchin*. Since the third century it was regarded as improper to effect a betrothment without a previous engagement. (1)

b. THE MODES BY WHICH THE BETROTHMENT WAS EFFECTED.

§ 39.

It is a general theory of the Talmudic Law that no contract can be formed by mere consent of the parties, but the consent has to be manifested by a certain legally established act, or formality, in order to make the contract valid. (2) The same theory, with all its consequences, was applied, also, to the marriage contract which was concluded by the betrothal. The mere consent of the parties to marry each other is not sufficient to constitute a betrothment, *i. e.*, the marriage contract; but a certain act, or formality, is required by which the mutual consent is legally manifested. For this purpose there are two especial formalities, either of which gives legal validity to the marriage contract. One of these

---

(1) See Talm. Kiddushin, p. 12*b*; Maim. Ishuth III. 22; Eben Ha-Ezer XXVI. 4.

(2) Maim. H. Mechera I. 1; II. 8; VII. 8, 9.

formalities is termed *Kaseph* (*i. e.*, money), the other *Sh'tar* (*i. e.*, a written instrument). [1]

The betrothal by *Kaseph* consisted in this, that the man gave, in the presence of two witnesses, to his chosen bride, a piece of money (even a *Peruta*, the smallest copper coin used in Palestine, was sufficient for that purpose), or any object of equal value, with the words: "Be thou consecrated (wedded) to me." [2]

---

[1] The Talmudic Law speaks, besides, of another mode by which, under certain conditions, marriage is legally contracted, namely, *Be-ah* (*i. e.*, *copulatio carnalis*). But this rather too primitive mode of contracting marriage was already in ancient times declared morally objectionable, and even punishable. Tal. Kiddushin, p. 12, Maim. Issure Be-ah XXI. 14; Eben Ha-Ezer XXVI. 4.

[2] Maim. Ishuth III. 1; Eben Ha-Ezer XXVII. 1.—The formality of contracting marriage by means of a piece of money did probably not originate before the time of Herodes; this is evident from the circumstance that the schools of Shamai and Hillel still differed as to the minimum value which that piece of money must have (Mishna Kidd. I. 1). In the apocryphal book of Tobit the act of contracting a marriage is occasionally described (chap. vii.), but no mention of that formality is made, though the whole tone of the narrative bespeaks a late time of its composition. It is not improbable that the formality was adopted from the Roman Law, in which a similar formality was established as one of the three modes of forming a legal marriage. The formality—there termed *coemptio*—is described in the following way (see Bouvier's Law Dict., art. "Coemptio"): "The parties met and gave each other a small sum of money. They then questioned each other in turn. The man asked the woman if she wished to be his *mater-familias*. She replied that she so wished. The woman then asked the man if he wished to be her *pater-familias*. He replied that he so wished. They then joined hands. And these were called nuptials by *coemptio*." The rabbinical formality differs, however, from the Roman in this, that the act is done by the man only; *he* gives the money or its value, and *he* speaks the formula, while her consent is expressed by her silent acceptance of both. This passivity on her side is in consequence of the Talmudic principle based on the expression used in the Mosaic Law: "IF A MAN TAKETH A WIFE;" "he takes and she *is* taken; he is the active and she the passive party." Talm. Kiddushin 2*b* and 5*b*.

As the formality of contracting marriage by money had in the Rabbinical Law merely a symbolical character, a coin of the least value, and even any other object representing such a value, could be used to perform this formality.

The formula, "Be thou consecrated (wedded) to me," could also be replaced by other words expressing the same idea, as: "Be thou my betrothed," "Be my wife," "Be mine," etc. The first-mentioned formula was generally used, and was later increased by the additional words: "According to the Law of Moses and Israel." (¹)

The betrothal by *Sh'tar* consisted in giving to the bride a WRITTEN INSTRUMENT containing the formula before mentioned, instead of a piece of money or its value, the same formalities being observed. This mode of betrothal seems, however, to have been resorted to only under extraordinary circumstances, as the former mode prevailed. (²)

During the Middle Ages it became customary for the act of betrothal by *Kaseph* to be performed by means of a plain RING, instead of a piece of money, (³) and

---

(¹) See R. M. ISSERLES' gloss to Eben Ha-Ezer XXVII. 1. The addition, כדת משה וישראל, is already mentioned in Thosifta Kethuboth IV. as having been used in the written marriage contracts (*Kethuboth*) at the time of Hillel, but it was not before the twelfth century that these words were generally added to the formula of betrothal. Compare FRANKEL's *Grundlinien*, p. XXV., note 4, and *Ben Chananja* III., p. 219.

(²) Maim. Ishuth III. 21.

(³) Mention of the wedding ring is made neither in the Talmud nor in the earlier rabbinical writings, which proves its later origin. The French and German rabbis of the thirteenth and the sixteenth centuries mention it as an established custom. See Tosaphoth Kidd. p. 9*a*, and gloss to Eben Ha-Ezer XXVII.—In the Christian Church the wedding ring was used much earlier, as it is already mentioned by the Fathers of the Church. Thus, ISIDOR HISPALEN (De offic. ecclesiast.

this custom has ever since prevailed up to our time, in which the plain circle of pure gold is generally looked upon as a symbol of conjugal fidelity, and as a reminder that the love of married people should be infinite. (¹)

c. BETROTHAL THROUGH REPRESENTATIVES.

§ 40.

The presence of the parties at the act of betrothment was not absolutely necessary, as either of them could be represented by an agent, appointed for that purpose. In this case the formula of the betrothment had to be changed according to the circumstances. It was, however, regarded more proper that the parties be present in person. (²)

d. WITNESSES.

§ 41.

The presence of two competent and qualified witnesses is an absolute requirement for the validity of the act of

---

II. 20) symbolizes the ring in the following way: "Illud vero quod imprimis annulus a sponso sponsae datur, fit hoc vel propter mutuæ fidei signum, vel propter it magis, ut eodem pignore eorum corda jungantur." The church probably adopted the custom from the ancient Romans, who, according to PLINY, hist. nat., lib. XXXIII., c. 5, made use of an iron wedding ring (*annulus pronubus*) as a symbol of strength and duration. See *Ben Chananja* X., p. 420, note 11.

(¹) A modern English writer, in speaking of the wedding ring, remarks: "The reason why a ring was pitched upon for the pledge, rather than anything else, was because anciently the ring was a seal, by which all orders were signed, and things of value secured, and therefore the delivery of it was a sign that the person to whom it was given was admitted into the highest friendship and trust. For this reason it was adopted as a ceremony in marriage to denote that the wife, in consideration of being espoused to the man, was admitted as a sharer in her husband's counsels, and a joint partner in his honor and estate." WILLIAM JONES, *Finger Ring Lore* (London, 1877), p. 297.

(²) Maim. Ishuth III. 19; Eben Ha-Ezer XXXV.

betrothal. No compliance with forms is, according to Jewish Law, of any avail when such witnesses are not present. According to the Talmudic Law, only males who are of age, of sound mind and of moral character, are, in general, regarded as competent to act as witnesses. Besides, the witnesses may be closely related neither to each other nor to either of the parties to the marriage. Persons suspected of unchastity are strongly objected to. (1)

As some rigorous rabbis objected even to persons not observing the Ritual Laws, the Israelitish Synod of Augsburg found it necessary to pass the following resolution: "No person can be rejected as witness to marriage and divorce on account of not observing the Ritual Laws." (2)

e. DOUBTFUL BETROTHMENT.

§ 42.

A betrothment in regard to whose validity any doubt arises, be it on account of an irregularity in the mode of its conclusion or on account of incompetency of the witnesses, or on account of stipulated conditions which have not been fulfilled, is either to be concluded anew according to the prescribed formalities or to be dissolved by a formal divorce. (3)

---

(1) Maim. Ishuth IV. 6; Eben Ha-Ezer XLII. 2-5, and gloss to the last paragraph. Regarding the general qualifications of the witnesses, see Maim. Eduth IX. and XIII.

(2) Verhandlungen der Zweiten Synode, p. 62-71.

(3) Maim. Ishuth IV. 6; Eben Ha-Ezer XLII. 5.

f. BENEDICTION OF BETROTHAL.

§ 43.

The ritual law of the Talmud requires that a benediction be pronounced at the betrothment. The benediction, termed *Berchath Kiddushin* or *Arusin*, expresses the Lord's praise because of the regulation and sanctification of the matrimonial relation. Besides, it alludes to the law that the betrothed parties are not permitted to enter upon the conjugal life before their union has been completed by the ceremonies of the nuptials. ([1])

The legal validity of the betrothal is by no means affected by the omission of that benediction.

B. NUPTIALS.

a. INTERVAL BETWEEN THE TWO ACTS.

§ 44.

Between the betrothal and the nuptials an interval elapsed, varying, in the Talmudic times, from a month for widows to a full year for virgins. ([2]) This interval was principally for the purpose of making the bride's outfit and the necessary preparation for the nuptials. During this period she lived with her friends, and every intimate intercourse between herself and her future husband was strictly prohibited. ([3])

([1]) Talm. Kethuboth 7; Maim. Ishuth III. 24; Eben Ha-Ezer XXXIV. 1.

([2]) Kethuboth, p. 57.

([3]) Maim. Ishuth X. 1; Eben Ha-Ezer LV. 1.

b. TERM AND ESSENCE OF THE CEREMONIES.

§ 45.

The nuptials are termed *Chuppa* or *Nissu-in*. The latter term means, literally, *taking* (namely, the wife). *Chuppa* originally denoted the bridal chamber, or the nuptial apartment, usually in the young husband's house, to which he conducted his bride, and around which the festivities of the occasion took place during the first seven days of their conjugal life. (¹) In later times, the word *Chuppa* denoted the *baldachin*, under which the ceremonies of solemnizing marriage took place. (²) Some authorities take the term in a rather figurative meaning, denoting the first intimate interview (*yichud*) between the bridegroom and bride. (³)

The nuptials have ever been attended with many kinds of ceremonies, which varied in different ages and countries. The essence of the ceremonies consisted in the act of conducting the bride from her home to that of the bridegroom, or a place representing his home. By this act, indicating that she was now placed under his marital authority and that they now commenced to live together as husband and wife, the marriage was regarded as having been consummated. They were then, in all respects, considered as husband and wife, though no conjugal intercourse had actually taken place. (⁴)

---

(1) Ps. xix. 6; Joel ii. 16. In this meaning the term was still used during the Talmudic period.

(2) Eben Ha-Ezer LV. 1, gloss.

(3) Maim. Ishuth X. 1.

(4) Talm. Kethuboth, p. 48; Maim. Ishuth X. 2; Eben Ha-Ezer LXI. 1. Also the Roman Law requires the *deductio in domum mariti*, or a place representing his home, to complete the marriage. Compare L. 5 D. de R. N.; L. 5 de usu et habit. 7, 8.

c. RELIGIOUS CEREMONIES.

§ 46.

The religious ceremonies attending the nuptials consist mainly in the recital of certain benedictions established by the Ritual Law for that occasion. In contradistinction to the *Berchath Arusin*—the Benediction of the Betrothal—these benedictions are termed *Berchoth Nissu-in*—Nuptial Benedictions. They refer to the divine origin of marriage, and invoke God's blessing upon the young couple. The presence of at least ten persons is required at the recital of these benedictions, in order to give the act publicity and solemnity. ([1])

Although a marriage is legally valid without the benedictions at the betrothal and nuptials, ([2]) still a marriage without such a ritual is of the rarest occurrence among Hebrews, as some religious ceremonies are generally regarded as highly appropriate to attend the act of concluding the most important and sacred relation of life.

The presence of a rabbi or minister is, according to the Talmudic Law, not required at the betrothal or the nuptials. The prescribed benedictions were pronounced either by the bridegroom or by any of the friends present. Such was also the custom during the Middle Ages. The intervention of a rabbi was necessary only in cases where a doubt arose concerning the validity of the concluded marriage. Subsequently, however, it became a settled rule to have the assistance of a rabbi in order

---

([1]) Talm. Kethuboth, pp. 7 and 8; Maim. Ishuth X. 3-5; Eben Ha-Ezer LXII. 1-4.

([2]) Maim. *ibid.* X. 6; Eben Ha-Ezer LV. 3 and LXI. 1, gloss.

to supervise that important act. In modern times it is generally regarded as a privilege of the rabbi or the authorized minister to solemnize the marriages within his congregation.

d. COMBINATION OF BETROTHAL AND NUPTIALS.

§ 47.

The interval between the betrothal and the nuptials having probably been found to lead to some inconvenience, it has since the sixteenth century become a general rule to join the act of betrothal with the ceremonies of the nuptials on the wedding day. By this combination, the act of concluding marriage received more solemnity and impressiveness. The joint act took place usually under the *nuptial baldachin*, which represented the ancient *Chuppa*—the bridal chamber. It was also customary to introduce the ritual of the act of betrothal and that of the nuptials with a benediction over a cup of wine,(¹) as a symbol of joy, and finally to let both the bridegroom and the bride drink out of that cup, which, in modern time, is usually symbolized as an indication of their willingness henceforth to drink together from the cup of life whatever Providence may allot to them.

e. KETHUBA.

§ 48.

In order to protect the wife in the event of her becom-

---

(1) See Eben Ha-Ezer LXII. 9.—That the combination of betrothal and nuptials occasionally occurred also in former centuries, is evident from Tosafoth Pesachim, p. 102b.

ing widowed or divorced, it was established by the Jewish Law that, before the nuptials, the husband was to make out an obligation in writing, which entitled her to receive a certain sum from his estate in the case of his death or in the case of her divorcement. This obligation was termed *Kethuba* (the marriage deed).

As minimum of this obligation was fixed the sum of two hundred silver *denarii* at the marriage of a virgin and one hundred at the marriage of a widow. This amount could, in either case, be increased at the option of the husband, which increase was termed *Thosaphoth Kethuba*—additional obligations.

For the security of the wife's claim to the amount fixed in the *Kethuba*, all the property of the husband, both real and personal, was mortgaged.

The institution of the *Kethuba* was originated or regulated by SIMON BEN SHATACH, President of the Sanhedrin in Jerusalem (about 100 B. C.). [1]

In later times, the document of the *Kethuba* was to contain, also, some articles of marriage settlements, setting forth the general duties of the husband to his wife, and stating the amount of value of the portion she brings to him in marriage, which amount, with an addition of fifty per cent., she was to receive in case her husband died or divorced her.

As all legal documents of the ancient rabbis, so also that of the *Kethuba* was formulated in the Aramaic language, and had to be signed by two witnesses.

---

[1] Tal. Kethuboth, p. 82b; Sabbath, p. 14.

The *Kethuba* is also mentioned in the book of Tobit, VII. 14, where it is termed *Syngraphe*.

f. FORM OF THE KETHUBA.

§ 49.

The following is a translation of the original form of the *Kethuba:* (1)

"On ——— (day of the week) the — day of the month ———, in the year ——— A. M., according to the Jewish reckoning, here, in the city of ———, Mr. ———, son of ———, said to the virgin ———, daughter of ———: 'Be thou my wife, in accordance with the laws of Moses and Israel, and I will work for thee, and I will hold thee in honor and will support and maintain thee, in accordance with the customs of Jewish husbands, who work for their wives, hold them in honor and support and maintain them. I will furthermore set aside the sum of two hundred silver denarii to be thy dowry, according to the law, and besides, provide for thy food, clothing and necessaries, and cohabit with thee according to the universal custom.'

"Miss ———, on her part, consented to become his wife. The marriage portion which she brought from her father's house, in silver, gold, valuables, clothes, etc., amounts to the value of ———. Mr. ———, the bridegroom, consented to increase this amount, from his property, with the sum of ———, making, in all, ———. He furthermore declared: 'I take upon myself and my heirs the responsibility for the amount due according to this *Kethuba*, and of the marriage portion, and of the additional sum (by which I promised to increase it). so that all this shall be paid from the best part of my property, real and personal, such as I now possess or may hereafter acquire. All my property, even the mantle on my shoulders, shall be mortgaged for the security of the claims above stated, until paid, now and forever.'

"Thus, Mr. ———, the bridegroom, has taken upon himself the fullest responsibility for all the obligations of this *Kethuba*, as customary in regard to the daughters of Israel.

---

(1) The original form of this document is to be found in Maim. Hil. Yibbum IV. 33; also in the book Nachlath Shib'a, which treats of all kinds of legal documents established by the rabbis.

and in accordance with the strict ordinances of our sages of blessed memory: so that this document is not to be regarded as an illusory obligation or as a mere form of documents.

"In order to render the above declarations and assurances of the said bridegroom, ———, to the said bride, ———, perfectly valid and binding, we have applied the legal formality of symbolical delivery.

"[Signature of the Groom.]

"[Signature of the two witnesses.]"

g. FORMER IMPORTANCE OF THE KETHUBA.

§ 50.

As long as the ancient law prevailed, by which a man could divorce his wife against her will, the greatest importance was attached to the *Kethuba*. Her claims, to which she was entitled by this obligation, proved, in many cases, an effective means of protecting her against a rash and inconsiderate divorcement. (¹) It was, therefore, in general, regarded as indispensable that such a document be written in due form, before the parties entered into conjugal life. In some places, however, it was not deemed necessary to write a formal document, as the husband was regarded bound to the contracts of the *Kethuba*, though not made out in writing.

From the time when the husband's right of divorcing his wife against her will was restricted by the generally adopted decree of the Synod of R. Gershom (eleventh century), the *Kethuba* lost its former importance. (²) Nevertheless, it was retained as an ancient custom, and looked upon as a kind of formal marriage settlement.

(¹) Tal. Kethuboth, p. 11; Maim. Ishuth X. 7.

(²) See R. ISSERLES' gloss to Eben Ha-Ezer LXVI. 2.

As the wife, in our days, is sufficiently protected by the civil laws of the country, and in many cases also by special marriage settlements made in a more legal form, the *Kethuba* is generally regarded as an unnecessary, useless formality, and is almost entirely dispensed with.

CHAPTER XI.

THE FORM OF MARRIAGE IN OUR TIME.

1. THE MODERN MODE OF SOLEMNIZATION.

§ 51.

In the modern mode of solemnizing marriage, the essential elements of the combined acts of betrothal and nuptials are retained, though more or less modified. These essential elements are the placing of the wedding ring on the bride's finger by the bridegroom in the presence of two witnesses, and the recital of the established formula of betrothment by him, preceded by a benediction (*Berchath Arusin*) and followed by the nuptial benedictions (*Berchoth Nissu-in*). Some immaterial and obsolete ceremonies and usages, however, as the nuptial *baldachin*, the reading of the *Kethuba*, etc., are mostly done away with and replaced by other forms, corresponding better with the views and the taste of our days.

To the laudable innovations almost generally adopted in the nuptial ceremonial belong:

1. The introductory address by the officiating rabbi, in which he reminds the parties to the marriage of the importance of the step they are about to take, and of the

sacredness of the mutual duties which their new relation imposes upon them.

2. The question he puts to each of the parties, whether they, of a free will, consent to be united as husband and wife, and pledge themselves to fulfill their respective duties in love and faithfulness. This question is to be answered in the affirmative by each of the parties.

MINOR DIFFERENCES.

§ 52.

Regarding some points in the ceremonial, no perfect uniformity prevails in our time.

a. ONE OR TWO WEDDING RINGS.

While, according to the established custom, only ONE wedding ring is used, which the bridegroom places on the bride's finger (usually on the index of the right hand), while pronouncing the ancient formula of betrothal, some modern rabbis introduced the custom that, in addition to this act, also the bride on her part tenders a ring to the groom while pronouncing similar words. (¹) By this innovation it is intended to express the full equality of woman with man in the conjugal relation

---

(¹) The same difference in regard to the use of one or two rings is found to exist also among the various denominations of the Christian Church. While the Greek and the German Lutheran Churches generally adopted an exchange of rings, the English and the American Churches retained the Roman Catholic custom of using only one ring, which the man puts upon the fourth finger of the woman's left hand in pronouncing a formula which greatly resembles the Jewish. It runs: "WITH THIS RING I THEE WED, and with all my worldly goods I thee endow."

and in moral life, so that, just as he consecrates her to be his alone, so she consecrates him to be hers alone, in person and affection. The Rabbinical Conference of Philadelphia (1869) passed, in this respect, the following resolution:

"The bride shall no longer occupy a passive position in the marriage contract, but a reciprocal avowal should be made by the bridegroom and the bride, by pronouncing the same formula, accompanied by an exchange of rings." [1]

The question of using two wedding rings was discussed also in the Augsburg Jewish Synod (1871). The Synod, however, did not think it advisable to make this innovation obligatory, but only declared it to be permissible and optional. The resolution passed on this subject reads as follows:

"In the act of concluding marriage, after the bridegroom having given unto the bride a ring with the words, 'Be thou wedded to me by this ring,' it is permitted that the bride likewise give unto him such a ring with corresponding words." [2]

b. THE FORMULA OF THE WEDDING CEREMONY.

The established formula of the wedding ceremony is:

"*Hare at m'kuddesheth le b'taba-ath zu kedath Moshe v'Yisroel.*"

In literal translation:

"Be thou sanctified (wedded) to me by this ring, according to the law of Moses and Israel."

This formula is generally still used in the original language. Some modern rabbis, however, prefer to use

---

[1] Protokolle, p. 19 *sq.*
[2] Verhandlungen, pp. 30–49.

a corresponding formula in the vernacular. The Philadelphia Conference adopted for this purpose the formula: "Be thou consecrated to me according to the law of God." (¹)

c. THE RITUAL.

The established benedictions (the *Berchath Arusin* preceding and the *Berchoth Nissu-in* following the act of giving the ring) are, in general, retained in the Hebrew language, omitting only the references to Jerusalem. In the ritual of some reform congregations, those benedictions are replaced by new prayers in the vernacular. (²) Some modern rabbis have also done away with the custom of using a cup of wine at the marriage ceremony. This ancient custom, though certainly not essential, has received a beautiful symbolical meaning, which might recommend its preservation.

2. CIVIL MARRIAGE.

§ 53.

Under rabbinical autonomy and jurisdiction, a Jewish marriage was recognized as only then complete and lawful when contracted strictly according to the forms prescribed in the Talmudic Code. (³) In modern time,

---

(¹) Protokolle, pp. 22–25.

(²) The ancient Wedding Ritual is found in LEESER's Prayer Book, p. 216,. As to the modern Rituals used in the American Jewish congregations, see EINHORN's Prayer Book, German, p. 441; English, p. 351; HUEBSCH's Prayer Book I., p. 230; SZOLD AND JASTROW's Prayer Book for Domestic Service, p. 60.

(³) See Eben Ha-Ezer XXVI. 1.

Jewish marriages, like all other marriages, are generally placed under the authority of the civil laws of the country. No person has a right to solemnize a marriage unless duly authorized by these laws. In general, the ministers of the different religious corporations are invested with this authority, and by the statutory laws of several of the States of this country it is expressly provided "that all persons may celebrate their marriage according to the rules and principles of that religious society, church or denomination to which they belong." But the State laws permit, also, CIVIL MARRIAGE, that is, a marriage without any religious solemnity, contracted before a judge of any court of record or by a justice of the peace.

The modern rabbi will not hesitate to recognize the validity and sanctity of a marriage contracted in this civil way, though from a religious standpoint he may disapprove members of his flock treating the most sacred relation of life merely as a civil contract, by entering upon it without the consecration of impressive religious solemnities. In this spirit the Second Israelitish Synod, held in Augsburg (1871), on motion, passed the following resolution:

"The civil marriage has, according to the view of Judaism, perfect validity or sanction, provided that the Mosaic Laws of prohibited degrees (for instance, the marriage between aunt and nephew) are not violated. The religious solemnization, however, is required (urgently recommended) as a consecration befitting the dignity of marriage." [1]

---

[1] Verhandlungen, p. 106 and p. 257.

THE EFFECTS OF MARRIAGE.

CHAPTER XII.

THE OFFSPRING OF LAWFUL AND UNLAWFUL MARRIAGES.

§ 54.

In regard to hereditary succession, the Rabbinical Law makes no distinction between children born in lawful and those born in unlawful wedlock. Even the most opprobrious kind of bastard, a *mamzer*, though in social and religious respects ranking very low, was regarded a legitimate child, capable of inheriting his putative father. ([1])

The guiding principle, in this respect, seems to have been that, if the father did wrong to the child in occasioning it to be brought into the world in a shameful manner, this wrong must not be increased by depriving it of its heriditary rights. ([2])

But in regard to the RELIGIOUS *status* of the offspring, it was of consequence whether a marriage was valid and

---

([1]) See Talm. Yebamoth, p. 22, and Maimonides Nechaloth I. 7.

([2]) See FRANKEL, *Grundlinien*, p. xxi., note 6.—A different view is taken by modern laws, in which it is generally held that the qualities of husband and wife in lawful marriage must be possessed by the parents in order to make the offspring legitimate. In Virginia, however, it is provided by a statutory law, that the issue of marriages deemed null in law shall nevertheless be legitimate. See BOUVIER'S Law Dict., under "Legitimacy."

legal or not. In this respect, the following four rules are laid down in the Rabbinical Law : (¹)

1. Wherever a marriage is valid and entered into without violation of any law, the child follows the status of the father. (²)

For instance, it is, in general, lawful for a *Kohen* (that is, a descendant of the ancient priestly families, who formerly had certain religious prerogatives and duties) to intermarry with common Israelites. Hence the offspring of a *Kohen* is regarded a *Kohen*, though the mother be a common Israelite, while the offspring of a common Israelitish father is regarded as a common Israelite, though the mother be a descendant of a *Kohen*.

2. Wherever a marriage is not void, though entered into in violation of a prohibitory law, the child follows the inferior status of either of the parents. (³)

For instance, a *mamzer*, that is, one born in an incestuous or adulterous connection, and an Israelite, shall not intermarry. (⁴) Still, their marriage, if entered into, is not void, though voidable. Hence the offspring of such a marriage is regarded as a *mamzer* in either case, whether the father or the mother had that character.

3. Where the mother was incapable of contracting a valid marriage with her child's father, but capable of being married to others, that child is to be considered a mamzer.

This rule applies exclusively to the offspring of either

(¹) Mishna Kiddushin III. 12; Eben Ha-Ezer VIII. 1-5.

(²) Similar to this rule is the maxim of the Civil Law: *Cum legitimae nuptiae factae sunt, patrem liberi sequuntur.*—"A child born under a legitimate marriage follows the (social) condition of the father."

(³) Also this rule has an analogy in the Roman Law regarding the civil rights of the offspring of a *matrimonium non justum*. See Ulpian. in fragm. V. 18: *Lex Mensia ex alterutro peregrino natum deterioris parentis conditionem sequi jubet.*

(⁴) See above, p. 43.

an adulterous or any of the incestuous connections distinctly prohibited in the Mosaic Law. (Lev. xviii.)

4. Where, in either of the parents, absolutely no capacity to contract a (Jewish) marriage exists, the child follows the status of the mother. (¹)

The capacity to contract a JEWISH marriage is by the Rabbinical Law restricted to Israelites by birth, and to such Gentiles as have embraced Judaism. (²) Hence the children of a Jewish father and a non-Jewish mother are regarded as non-Jews, while those of a non-Jewish father and a Jewish mother are deemed Jews.

Although in modern time such intermarriages are legalized by the civil laws of the country, this rule, regarding the religious *status* of the offspring of a mixed parentage, is still generally adhered to in the Jewish community. The adherence to this rule is also recommended by the consideration that children, in their religious training, are mostly influenced by their mother.

(¹) The Mishna Kidd. III. 12 speaks only of cases of such incapacity on the MOTHER's side, but the Gemara and later rabbinical authorities decide that the rule applies as well to cases where the incapacity is on the FATHER's side: נכרי ועבד הבא על בת ישראל הולד כשר, Yebamoth, p. 45; Eben Ha-Ezer IV. 19.—The difference between the rule 3 and the rule 4 is obvious. There is a case of a MORAL CRIME (incest or adultery), in which both of the parents participated; hence their offspring becomes branded with the character of a *mamzer;* while the fourth rule refers to an incapacity based on purely religious considerations, which are binding only upon the Jewish party of the parents; hence their offspring is not considered a *mamzer.* [See the Rev. Dr. A. HUEBSCH's (Senior) article "*Puncto Mischehen,*" in *Die Deborah,* Vol. XXVII. No. 30.] That the child, in the latter case, follows the *status* of the mother, is in Talm. Kidd., p. 68b, based on Scriptural passages, but the underlying principle has an analogy in the maxim of the Civil Law: *Qui nascitur sine legitimo matrimonio, matrem sequitur.*"—"He who is born out of lawful marriage follows the condition of the mother." D. I. 5, 24.

(²) See above, p. 46.

CHAPTER XIII.

HUSBAND AND WIFE.

§ 55.

The marriage relation imposes on husband and wife certain obligations and confers upon them certain rights. These duties and rights are largely considered and very minutely regulated in the Rabbinical Law. (¹)

As the modern Jews, in all civilized countries, are, in this respect and in all purely civil affairs, entirely governed by the laws of those States whose citizens they are, we do not propose to enter here minutely into all the details of the Rabbinical regulations concerning this subject, but shall confine ourselves to the leading principles only regarding—

1. The marital duties and rights, and
2. The wife's property.

1. MARITAL DUTIES AND RIGHTS.

a. THE HUSBAND'S DUTIES.

§ 56.

The Mosaic Law contains no express provisions con-

(¹) Talm. Kethuboth, chapters IV-XIII.; Maim. Ishuth XII.-XXIII.; Eben Ha-Ezer LXIX.-CXVIII.

cerning the marital rights and duties, except the injunction made in a certain case: "Her FOOD, her RAIMENT and her CONJUGAL RIGHT shall he (the husband) not diminish." (Exodus xxi. 10.)

Upon this casual intimation are based the elaborate regulations of the Rabbinical Code concerning the husband's obligations, which are treated of under the following headings. It is his legal duty:

1. To furnish his wife with the necessaries of life, including—(*a*) food; (*b*) clothing; (*c*) dwelling.

2. To have conjugal cohabitation with her.

3. To provide suitable medical care and nursing when she is sick.

4. To protect her and to ransom her in the eventuality of her falling into captivity.

5. To provide for her burial in case of her death.

The extent of the obligations concerning her food, clothing and dwelling depends upon his fortune and situation in life, and also upon the local customs. If he become poor, she must be content with his modest way of living. In case of necessity, he is, according to some authorities, bound to hire himself out as a day laborer in order to gain the means of supporting his wife. (¹)

But a man of wealth is under obligation to maintain his wife according to his fortune, without regard to her lower situation in life before marriage. In this respect it is a Talmudic maxim: "The wife ascends with her husband, but she does not descend with him." That is to say, she is entitled to all the advantages of his stand-

---

(1) Eben Ha-Ezer LXX. 3.

ing in society, without losing those which she enjoyed in her parental home. (¹)

Generally, the wife is to receive her board in her husband's house, at his table, but in the case of her lawful absence it is his duty to provide her with the necessaries of life in that place where she abides. (²)

A husband neglecting to maintain his wife can be compelled by court to fulfill his duty.

If he deserted his wife without making provision for her support, the court adjudicated to her an alimony from his property. (³)

He is also liable for the refunding of amounts which she, in his absence, borrows for her actual support, on his account, though he had given public notice not to trust her. (⁴) But if a third man, of his own free will, furnishes a married woman, in the absence of her husband, with the necessaries of life, he has, to use the rabbinical phrase, "put his money on the horn of a deer," that is, he has lost his money, as he can not maintain an action at law against the husband for the outlay. (⁵)

---

(1) Talm. Kethuboth, p. 61.
(2) Eben Ha-Ezer LXX. 12 and gloss.
(3) Eben Ha-Ezer *ibid.* § 5, gloss.
(4) *Ibid.*, §§ 8 and 12, gloss.
(5) Mishna Kethuboth XIII. 2. It is added there, that the PRIESTLY COURT in Jerusalem (probably a kind of court of equity) differed on this point, holding the husband to be liable. As an interesting parallel to this difference of view between common courts and courts of equity regarding a similar case, as treated in modern times, we shall quote here the following from Bishop's Marriage and Divorce II. 612, fourth edition: "Money may buy necessaries, but it is not such in itself Therefore, if a man lends to a married woman, whose husband, being under obligation to furnish her necessaries, neglects so to do, money which she actually expends in this way, he can not maintain an action

The husband is not answerable for the wife's debts contracted before her marriage, nor for those which she incurred afterward without his authority. Nor is he liable for her torts and crimes. If she have no separate property, all judgments against her for debts, torts, fines, etc., remain a claim against her, which she is to pay from her dowry when becoming a widow or divorced. (¹)

The duty of conjugal cohabitation is legally, as well as ritually and ethically, regulated in the Rabbinical Code. A continued refusal, on either side, regarding this duty, if not excused by sickness and circumstances, offers a ground for divorce. (²)

Concerning the duty of ransoming the wife in the case of her falling into captivity, it must be borne in mind that the frequent invasions of Bedouins in the oriental countries and the continual wars in Europe during the Middle Ages made the express provision for such an eventuality quite necessary. The husband was in such

---

at law against the husband for the money. * * * But in equity—that is, in that form of legal proceeding which is carried on in a court of equity, in distinction from a court of common law—the person who lends money to the wife with which to buy necessaries, can recover the money, on showing that it has been so expended in fact."

(1) Eben Ha-Ezer XCI. 4; Choshen Mishpat, chapter 349, 1.—It must be remembered that, by the Jewish Law, the husband is merely a usufructuary of his wife's property; hence he can not be chargeable for her debts, torts, fines, etc. It is different in the modern, especially the common law, in which the principle is established by which "the husband and wife are regarded as one person, and her legal existence and authority in a degree lost or suspended, during the continuance of the matrimonial union." This principle vests in the husband whatever personal property belonged to the wife before marriage, and throws upon him, during coverture, all the obligations of the wife, so that he is answerable for her debts before coverture, and liable for all the torts and frauds of her committed during coverture. Compare Kent's Comm. II. 144–150.

(2) Kethub. 61–64; Maim. Ishuth XIV.; Eben Ha-Ezer LXXVI.

eventuality under obligation to ransom his wife, even at the expense of an amount far beyond that of her dowry. (¹)

The duty of providing for the wife's burial includes also that of providing for a tombstone and for funeral solemnities according to his and her standing in society. (²)

b. HIS LEGAL RIGHTS.

§ 57.

The husband's rights are, by the Jewish law, the following:

1. He is entitled to whatever she may earn by her labor and industry.

2. He is entitled to whatever she gains by chance.

3. He is entitled to the usufruct of all the property which she brought into marriage, as her portion, and of the property she during her coverture received by inheritance, donation, legacy or otherwise.

4. He becomes her sole heir on her death.

His right to her earnings is regarded as the consideration for his duty of supporting her. Hence, if she, of her own free will, renounces her claim of being supported by him, her earnings are her own and can be held free from the claims of her husband. But the husband can not compel her to live on her own earnings by such a settlement. (³)

(¹) Eben Ha-Ezer LXXVIII. 3.

(²) *Ibid.* LXXXIX.

(³) Eben Ha-Ezer LXIX. 4.

In this way the wife was protected against a husband squandering her earnings and against his niggardliness.

Regarding his right to the usufruct of her property, and to the succession to her estate on her death, we shall speak further under the heading, "The wife's property."

c. THE WIFE'S DUTIES AND RIGHTS.

§ 58.

On marriage, the wife takes the domicil of the husband. If he afterward changes his domicil, she is to follow him, but she can not be compelled to follow him into a foreign country where a different language is spoken. She can also object to his removing to another place which in sanitary respects or in regard to comfort is inferior to her present abode. But if it is impossible for him to make a living in his former place of residence, it is her duty to follow him. ([1])

It is, in general, the wife's duty to manage the household, to engage in the female work of domestic life, such as cooking, baking, sewing, etc. It belongs also to her duties to nurse her children, generally, herself. Even if able to keep many servants, she is not permitted to live in idleness, as "idleness leads to sin." Under all circumstances, she has personally to perform certain services of loving care for her husband's ease and comfort. ([2])

The rights of the wife are implied in the husband's duties, treated of above.

([1]) Talm. Kethuboth, p. 110; Maim. Ishuth XIII. 13; Eben Ha-Ezer LXXV.

([2]) Kethuboth, p. 69b; Maim. Ishuth XXI.; Eben Ha-Ezer LXXX.

By the Jewish law, the wife does not succeed to her husband's estate on his death, but receives the portion which she brought into marriage, and besides, the dowry fixed in the *Kethuba*. As long as the widow does not claim the amount of her dowry, and as long as she does not remarry, she has the right to remain in her deceased husband's house and be supported by his legal heirs in the same way as she was accustomed during his lifetime. (¹)

2. *THE WIFE'S PROPERTY.*

§ 59.

In the Rabbinical Law, the wife's property is divided into three classes, governed by different rules:

1. DOTAL PROPERTY (Hebrew, *Nedunja*), that is, her portion, consisting in money, goods or estate, which she brings to her husband in marriage. The total value of this property was usually mentioned in the marriage deed, with the express or implied understanding that the husband be responsible for this amount.

2. PARAPHERNAL PROPERTY, that is, whatever she either brings in marriage above the dotal property, and which she reserves for herself under her own responsibility, or the property which she, during marriage, acquires by inheritance or by gift, grant or bequest from any person other than her husband.

3. HER STRICTLY PRIVATE PROPERTY, that is, property which her husband donated to her during marriage, or which a third person donated to her with the express

---

(¹) Maim. Ishuth XIX. 21; Eben Ha-Ezer XCIII. 4 and gloss.

condition that it be exclusively for her own use for certain purposes.

(*a*) Dotal property vests in the husband as trustee for the wife. He is entitled, however, during marriage, to take and use the rents, fruits and profits thereof. His are also its betterments. But he is responsible for the loss, damage and deterioration of that property. At the dissolution of marriage by his death, or by divorce, it is to be returned to her in that condition in which it was, or with that value which it had at the time when vested in him. In contradistinction to the second class, this property is termed, in the Talmudic Law, *Tson Barzel* (*pecus ferreum*)—property of iron sheep, as it was like sheep, from which profit (the wool) is derived, and, on the other hand, it resembled iron, in so much, as its substance could not be destroyed nor its value deteriorated.

(*b*) Regarding the paraphernal property, the husband is likewise entitled to all the fruits and profits derived therefrom, but he is not responsible for its loss and deterioration. Upon his death, or in case of divorce, this property returns to her in that state in which it is found at that time.

The Talmudic term for such property is *Nechse Melug*—property of simple usufruct.

(*c*) The property characterized as the wife's separate estate is beyond her husband's control, and the rents and profits thereof are not subject to his disposal. She is, however, not permitted to alienate the substance of property which the husband donated to her during marriage, as he is entitled to inherit it on her death. ([1])

([1]) Eben Ha-Ezer LXXXV. 7.

The wife being the owner, and the husband the usufructuary of the dotal and paraphernal property, it is not subject to the debts of the husband, nor liable to be taken in execution for her debts or damages. Such property can be sold or transferred to third persons only with the joint consent of both husband and wife.

The husband is permitted to sell his usufruct of that property, but for a limited time only.

In any lawsuit against third persons concerning the substance of such property, the husband needs a power of attorney from his wife to act in her name. Such power of attorney is, however, not required where the action concerns the profits of the property only. (¹)

Upon the wife's death, the husband becomes, by the Talmudic Law, the sole heir of all her property, the dotal and paraphernal as well as her separate property. This refers, however, only to property of which she was in actual possession at the time of her death, but not to property in expectancy, which falls to her descendants, or, in the absence of such, to her nearest relation. This Talmudic Law was modified in the twelfth century. Several distinguished rabbis of France and Lombardy, under the celebrated R. JACOB BEN MEIR (Rabenu Tam), enacted the law providing that, when the wife dies childless within the first year after marriage, the whole amount of her dotal property is to be returned to her father or his legal heirs. To this the Jewish congregations of Spire, Worms and Mainz subsequently added the provision that, if the wife dies childless in the second year after marriage, half of the dotal, and, according to some au-

---

(¹) Eben Ha-Ezer, *ibid.*, § 4.

thorities, also half of the paraphernal property, is to be returned to her relations. This provision (termed תקנת שו"ם) became, later, an established rule among the German Jews. (¹)

(¹) The particulars concerning the wife's property and the husband's right of inheritance are to be found in Eben Ha-Ezer, chapters LXXXV.-XCII. See also MOSES MENDELSSOHN's *Ritualgesetze der Juden betreffend Erbschaften, Testamente und Ehesachen*. Berlin, 1787.

DISSOLUTION OF MARRIAGE.

A legally valid marriage is dissolved either—
1. By the death of one of the parties, or
2. By divorce.

CHAPTER XIV.

DISSOLUTION BY DEATH.

§ 60.

In order to establish the dissolution of a marriage by death, so that the surviving party be permitted to remarry, death must be proved beyond any doubt. Great difficulties often arise in this respect in cases where, for instance, the husband died abroad, or where he was lost by an accident. The difficulty in ascertaining the actual death of a person was naturally still greater in former times, when the means of communication and investigation were not as developed as in our days. The Talmudic Law is very minute in its regulations providing for such cases. (¹)

---

(1) See Talm. Yebamoth, chapters X., XV. and XVI.; Maim. Gerushin XII. 15—XIII. 29; Eben Ha-Ezer XVII. 3–58. In the rabbinical provisions concerning this subject, only the case of the absent HUSBAND's death is considered, because he, on account of his usual pur-

a. THE EVIDENCE OF DEATH.

§ 61.

The following are the leading principles of the rabbinical provisions regarding the evidence of death:

The death of the absent husband must with certainty be proved either — (1) by the testimony of persons who witnessed either his demise or his funeral, or (2) by an unmistakable identification of his dead body.

The testimony to the death must be of such a nature as to exclude every possibility of mistake. A testimony based solely upon circumstantial evidence, or upon mere conjecture and presumption, is of no value. If, for instance, the husband was known to have been on board a ship which was wrecked at sea, his death is not sufficiently proved by this fact, as he might have been saved by another ship which was passing. In a smaller body of water, however, the boundaries of which are within the reach of the eyes, the evidence that the boat perished and no one on it was seen to be saved, is sufficient to establish the death. A report that the husband died in a battle, if not corroborated by the evidence that he was actually buried, is no sufficient proof to permit the wife to remarry, as in the confusion of a battle field a mere trance caused by severe wounds might have been mistaken for actual death. (¹)

---

suits, happens oftener to be abroad and on journeys. Besides, it must be remembered that the Talmudic Law still had polygamous institutions in view, in which the husband's death was of greater legal consequence than the wife's, in regard to a contemplated remarriage of the surviving party. Compare FRANKEL's *Grundlinien*, p. 40, note 2.

(1) Eben Ha-Ezer XVII. § 32.

b. THE WITNESSES TO THE DEATH.

§ 62.

Concerning the witnesses testifying to a husband's death, the Talmudic Law is not as strict as in regard to testimony in general. In this respect, there is a rabbinical maxim: "Some allowance is to be made in favor of the unfortunate woman, who otherwise would have to remain in eternal widowhood." (¹) While in all criminal and civil cases, and in all matrimonial affairs, it was an established rule of law that "everything must be proved by two witnesses," the testimony of a single witness was considered sufficient in this instance, since in most cases it would be impossible to find two witnesses to prove the death of the absent husband. Besides, the one witness could not be presumed to testify falsely in this instance, as he must expect that the possible return of the still living husband would clearly demonstrate the falsehood of that testimony. (²)

Also the testimony of a woman, or of near relatives, and of other persons otherwise regarded as incompetent witnesses by the Rabbinical Law, can be admitted to establish the death of an absent person. Excluded from such testimony are, however, persons mentally deranged, and besides, such persons as are presumed to have a spite against the unfortunate woman, since they might intend to bring her into difficulties by a false report of her husband's death. (³)

(¹) משום עיגונא אקילו בה רבנן. Talm. Yebamoth, p. 88.

(²) Maim. Gerushin XII. 15 and XIII. 29.

(³) Talm. Yebamoth, p. 113; Maim. Gerushin XII. 16; Eben Ha-Ezer XVII. 4.

Under certain circumstances, even hearsay evidence, as well as written statements, though otherwise not accepted in the Jewish law, are admitted as sufficient proof of a person's death.

C. CONSEQUENCES OF A PREMATURE REMARRIAGE.

§ 63.

If the husband whose death had been believed returns after his wife's remarriage, she is to leave her first husband as well as the second one. Besides, she forfeits her dowry (*Kethuba*) from the first and the second husband, and her children born in that second marriage are regarded as born in adultery. [1]

In view of these disastrous consequences of a premature remarriage, the wife had to be very careful not to

---

[1] Tal. Yebamoth, p. 87b; Maim. Gerushin X. 5; Eben Ha-Ezer XVII. 56.—The supposed evidence of the first husband's death having thus been proved to be false, it did not dissolve the first marriage; hence the second marriage is void, and to be regarded merely as an adulterous connection. But neither can the first marriage be continued, as by the Jewish Law no man is permitted to continue to live with his wife after her having committed adultery (see above, p. 27). Although the law just quoted refers only to VOLUNTARY adultery, still its rigor was also applied to the present case, in order to punish the woman for her over-hasty remarriage.

In American courts it has been ruled that, to justify a second marriage by the wife, there must be a general report of the husband having died at some particular PLACE, and by some particular MEANS, as by shipwreck, which the report SPECIFIES.

By the statutory law of some of the United States it is provided that. if a husband or wife, upon any false rumor, in appearance well founded, of the death of the other, when such other has been absent seven years (according to some statutes, five, or even two years), shall marry again, he or she shall not be liable to the pains of adultery (or bigamy); but the second marriage is under all circumstances void; the former marriage, however, remains in force. See KENT's Comm. II. 79; BISHOP's Marriage and Div. (fourth edition), I. §§ 298 and 710.

contract a second marriage before having used every means to ascertain, beyond any doubt, that her former husband was actually dead. For this reason, the statement of a wife before a court that her absent husband died abroad was accepted so as to permit her to enter a new marriage. Her statement was, however, not credited, in case she was known to have lived in disharmony and quarrel with her husband, or where her statement appeared to rest on mere conjecture. ([1])

d. IDENTIFICATION.

§ 64.

Regarding the identification of the corpse of one who had been killed by an accident, the Rabbinical Law is very strict. Only infallible signs on the body found, such as the distinctly recognizable features in the not yet decomposed face, or remarkable abnormities of the limbs, are admitted as proofs of identity. Other marks on the body, or garments and objects found on the same, are not regarded as sufficient to establish the identity. ([2])

e. ABSENT AND NOT HEARD OF.

§ 65.

The circumstance of a person being absent for a long period of time without having been heard of, is by the Jewish law no evidence of his death, such as to entitle the wife to remarry, since nothing but actual death, or

---

([1]) Talm. Yebamoth, p. 114b; Maim. Gerushin XIII. 1-5; Eben Ha-Ezer XVII. 43.

([2]) Maim. Gerushin XIII. 21, 22; Eben Ha-Ezer XVII. 22-28.

a divorce by the husband, can dissolve the marriage tie. (¹)

f. RESOLUTIONS OF RABBINICAL CONFERENCES.

§ 66.

Modern rabbis are generally of the opinion that the Talmudic rules concerning the evidence of death are somewhat obsolete, being in some respects defective and insufficient for our time, in which the ways and means of ascertaining the death or the whereabouts of a lost person, or of establishing the identity of a found body, are made so much easier and surer. The Rabbinical Conference of Philadelphia, as well as the Jewish Synod of Augsburg, passed resolutions to the effect that the question as to whether a lost person is to be regarded as dead or not, is to be left entirely to the decision of the competent courts of the country.

The resolution of the Philadelphia Conference reads as follows:

(¹) See FRANKEL's *Grundlinien*, p. 41.

By the laws of some European countries, for instance, Prussia (*Landrecht*, Th. II., Tit. 1, §§ 665, 666), the wife is permitted to remarry, if by a judicial decision the husband is declared to be dead. Such a declaration of death can be obtained, if nothing has been heard from the absent husband within ten years (*ibid.*, Th. II., Tit. 18, § 823.)

Here, in the American States, it is generally held that the proof of an absence of seven years (in New Hampshire three years), and the party not having been heard of, gives rise to the presumption of death. This presumption does not, however, entitle the remaining party to remarry, but it is a ground for a judicial divorce. Without such a divorce the second marriage, though contracted in good faith, after the lapse of this period, would be a nullity, in case the absent party should be shown afterward to be living. But if there had been a divorce for the cause of absence, the second marriage would be valid, whether the absent one were truly living or dead. See BISHOP's Mar. and Div. (4th edition) I., § 824.

"The decision of the question, whether the husband or the wife is to be declared dead or lost, is to be left to the courts." (1)

The resolution unanimously passed in the Second Jewish Synod of Augsburg reads:

"A final decision of the courts concerning the identity of a dead person, and a judicial decision declaring the lost person to be dead, have also sanction for ritual cases." (2)

---

(1) Protokolle, p. 37.
(2) Verhandlungen, pp. 114–127.

CHAPTER XV.

DIVORCE.

1. *INTRODUCTORY.*

§ 67.

Divorce is the legal dissolution of the marriage relation while both parties are still alive.

The ethical principle of marriage is certainly against such a dissolution. This principle demands that those who enter into the conjugal covenant should regard it as a relation permanent as their own lives. The very words of Scripture, in speaking of the original institution of marriage — "Man shall cleave to his wife, and they shall be one flesh" (Gen. ii. 24) — intimate that marriage shall be an indissoluble union. But the ethical principle is not always sufficient for life's actual circumstances. There are circumstances the evil influences of which sometimes undermine the very basis of a contracted marriage, and defeat its purposes to such a degree as to render the continuation of this relation unadvisable and almost impossible. When, through the fault of one of the parties, the matrimonial union has suffered a breach which can not be healed; when mutual love and affection, harmony and peace have been banished from their hearts and their home, and constant discord and strife and mutual aversion and animosity imbitter domestic life; in one word, when, instead of being a source of the highest felicity, marriage becomes the source of the deepest woe and misery; then the sanctity of matrimony, as well as the welfare of the parties, make it advisable that the unhappy union should be dissolved. Divorce is here only the external dissolution of a relation which, internally, has already been destroyed.

The Mosaic Law, which, though raising the highest standard of moral principles, never loses sight of life as it is, and endeavors to regulate and mitigate such evils as can not be extirpated, therefore permits divorces under certain conditions.

2. REGULATIONS OF THE MOSAIC LAW.

§ 68.

The principal passage concerning divorce is found in Deuteronomy xxiv. 1, 2, and reads as follows:

"When a man hath taken a wife, and married her, and it come to pass that she find no favor in his eyes, because he hath found some uncleanness in her: then let him write her a bill of divorcement, and give in her hand, and send her out of his house. And when she is departed out of his house, she may go and become another man's wife." ([1])

---

[1] In close connection follows here the law prohibiting the former husband to remarry the divorced woman after she had contracted another marriage, which again had been dissolved. This part of the law was treated of above, in the chapter on prohibited marriages, p. 42, § 13.

The Septuagint and some modern commentators regard the four verses of this passage as forming only one sentence, of which the first three are the conditional clauses (*protasis*), while verse 4 is the main clause (*apodosis*), and consequently translate: "*If a man has taken a*

In the law before us the permission to dissolve the marriage relation is given under two restrictions:

1. It shall not depend upon the whim or caprice of the husband to put his wife away, but he must give certain reasons for doing so. It is not sufficient that "she finds no favor in his eyes," but there must be a certain cause justifying this disfavor; he must have "found some uncleanness in her."

2. He shall not put her away without ceremony, by mere word of the mouth, but by a formal act; a bill of divorcement must be written, which he must give into her hand before sending her away from his house. The object of requiring this formal document was, obviously, to prevent passionate haste in divorce. In those ancient times, when the art of writing was not as general as in our days, the preparation of such a written document would require the intervention of a priest or magistrate skilled in this art. In this way, a certain delay and opportunity for reconsideration were secured, and the priest or magistrate conducting the act was expected to exercise his influence to reconcile the parties, if possible, and to prevent false and frivolous complaints from being treated as grounds for divorce. (¹) Besides, the written document

---

wife," etc., "and given her a bill of divorcement; and (v. 2) if she has departed out of his house and become another man's wife; and (v. 3) if the latter husband hate her," etc., "then (v. 4) her former husband may not take her again to be his wife," etc. According to this translation, the passage before us neither institutes nor enjoins divorce, but assumes that in putting away a wife it was an old custom to have a written document of divorcement. But however the words of this passage are taken, they involve the permission of divorce and establish the old custom as a law.

(1) See SAALSCHUETZ, *Das Mosaische Recht*, p. 801, and note on Deut. xxiv., in SPEAKER's Comm. on the Pentateuch.

was to serve as a certificate in the hand of the divorced woman that she was free to contract a second marriage.

In two cases, elsewhere provided for in the law, the husband was altogether deprived of the right of divorce, namely, if he had accused his newly-married wife of ante-nuptial unchastity, and the charge, on investigation, had been found to be slanderous (Deut. xxii. 13–19); and in case he had seduced her before marriage (*ibid.* xxii. 28, 29).

No mention is made in the Mosaic Law whether also the wife had a right of divorce on her side, in case she was the complaining party. This omission is, as will be seen further on, supplied by the traditional law, which provides for cases in which the wronged wife could enforce a divorce. But even in such cases the final dissolution of marriage could be effected only by a bill of divorce which the husband, though under compulsion, handed or sent to his wife, since it was regarded as against the letter and the spirit of the law that a woman should dismiss her husband by giving him such a bill. (¹)

3. *RABBINICAL INTERPRETATION AND PROVISIONS.*

§ 69.

The interpretation of the expression, "some unclean-

(¹) Josephus, Antiqu. XV. 7, 10, and XVIII. 5, 4, mentions two examples of a woman giving a divorce to her husband; one was Salome, the sister of Herod, and the other Herodias, the daughter-in-law of that King. But in the former case it is expressly stated that "this was not according to the Jewish law." In this, as in other respects, the Herodians followed the Roman custom, which permitted such divorces. From Juvenal VI. 229, 230, and Martial VI. 7, we see to what moral corruption this custom led in Rome.

ness" (Hebrew, *Ervath dabar*—literally, "the nakedness or shame of a thing"), used in the Mosaic Law as the ground of divorce, is a point on which the schools of Shammai and Hillel, flourishing in the last century of the Second Jewish Commonwealth, widely differed. The former school took that expression in an ethical sense, and consequently limited the husband's right of divorce to the case of a moral delinquency or unchaste demeanor in the woman; while the school of Hillel, understanding the expression to relate to anything offensive and displeasing, permitted divorce for any cause that might disturb domestic peace. (¹)

In legal respects, the opinion of the school of Hillel prevailed; but divorce was morally disapproved of by the rabbis in general. This disapproval found expression in the two sentences: "He who divorces his wife is hated before the Lord," and "Tears are shed on God's altar for the one who forsakes the wife of his youth."

For the protection of woman, several rules were adopted which prevented inconsiderate divorces. Such a preventive was, in many cases, the institution of the *Kethuba*, which secured to the wife a certain dowry in the case of divorce, as also in the case of the husband's death. (²)

(¹) Talm. Gittin 90a. The interpretation of the Hillelites is supported by the circumstance that the expression "*Ervath dabar*" also occurs in the preceding chapter (xxiii. 13) in regard to CAMP LIFE, where it clearly has the general meaning of anything which is disgusting and unbecoming. The highly noble and humane tendencies of the founder and followers of this school are too well known to permit us to ascribe this, their extension of the causes of divorce, to a loose view of the marriage relation. It seems, rather, that at a time of moral corruption that school deemed it necessary to extend the right of divorce in order to prevent a greater evil—the frequency of adultery. Compare L. PHILIPSON's *Israelitische Religionslehre*, III., p. 255.

(²) See above, page 88.

Also the numerous and minute regulations concerning the formalities in writing and handing over the document of divorce were mostly calculated to render the act difficult and prevent passionate haste on the part of the husband.

Besides, provisions were made to secure the rights of the wife, so as to entitle her to a divorce in certain cases.

4. RESTRICTION OF THE RIGHT OF DIVORCE.

§ 70.

In the eleventh century, Rabbi GERSHOM, one of the most celebrated rabbinical authorities of that time, to whom also the abolishment of the last vestiges of polygamy among the European Jews is ascribed, enacted the law interdicting the divorcing a wife against her will, except in certain cases, which will be specified further on. (¹)

There are by the Rabbinical Law four kinds of divorce, which in some respects are treated differently, though the form of the bill of divorcement is to be the same in all cases.

1. Divorce by mutual agreement of the parties. In this case the wife is entitled to receive the dowry fixed in the *Kethuba*.

2. Divorce enforced upon the wife on the petition of the husband. Whenever the court, after having examined the causes of the complaining husband, grants such a divorce, the wife, as the guilty party, forfeits her dowry.

3. Divorce enforced upon the husband on the petition

(¹) See R. MOSES ISSERLES' gloss to Eben Ha-Ezer CXIX. 6.

of the wife. When the causes of the complaining wife are found to be sufficient to entitle her to divorce, the husband is compelled to give her the bill of divorcement and to pay her dowry.

4. Divorce enforced by court, without petition of either of the parties. In certain cases, to be stated further on, the Jewish court compelled the husband to divorce his wife, though both parties desired to continue their marriage.

5. SPECIFIC CAUSES FOR DIVORCE.

With reference to the four kinds of divorce just mentioned, the specific causes may be set forth as follows:

a. MUTUAL AGREEMENT.

§ 71.

In the case of mutual agreement, no specific causes are required. According to a principle of the Rabbinical Law, the court has no right to interfere where both parties declare that their marriage is a failure, and that they have come to the conclusion to dissolve their unhappy and burdensome relation. (1)

---

(1) See FRANKEL's *Grundlinien des Mosaisch-Talmudischen Eherechts*, p. 44.—It is different in modern laws, which in general do not acknowledge the right of married persons to be their own judges of the causes for which divorce should be allowed them, "since the public and the children have interests in every marriage, as well as the parties." Divorce is, therefore, granted only on a complaint of one party against the other, made in due form, for a cause authorized by law and supported by due proof. Compare BISHOP's Mar. and Div. I. 40 and II. 236. According to the laws of some European countries, however, divorce may be granted on the consent of the parties if, after a year's separation from bed and board, a reconciliation proves to be impossible.

b. THE HUSBAND'S CAUSES.

§ 72.

The husband is entitled to divorce:

1. On account of the wife's adultery, and even on strong suspicion of her having committed this crime. (¹)

2. On account of her public violation of moral decency. (²)

3. On account of her change of religion or proved disregard of the Ritual Law in the management of the household, by which she caused him to transgress the religious precepts against his will. (³)

4. On account of obstinate refusal of connubial rights during a whole year. (⁴)

5. On account of her unjustified refusal to follow him to another domicile. (⁵)

6. On account of insulting her father-in-law in the presence of her husband, or for insulting the husband himself. (⁶)

7. On account of certain incurable diseases, rendering cohabitation impracticable or dangerous, as epilepsy, etc. (⁷)

---

(1) Eben Ha-Ezer CXV. 7.

(2) Tal. Kethuboth, p. 72; Eben Ha-Ezer CXV. 4 and CXIX. 4.

(3) Eben Ha-Ezer CXV. 1–4 and gloss.

(4) Eben Ha-Ezer LXXVII. 2 and gloss.

(5) Eben Ha-Ezer LXXV. 1.

(6) Eben Ha-Ezer CXV. 4.

(7) Eben Ha-Ezer CXVII. 1–11.

c. THE WIFE'S CAUSES.

§ 73.

The wife is entitled to be divorced:

1. On account of loathsome chronic diseases which the husband contracted after marriage, or

2. On account of a disgusting trade, in which he engaged after marriage, the same being of such a nature as to render cohabitation with him intolerable. (¹)

3. On account of repeated ill treatment received from her husband, as for beating her, or turning her out of doors, or prohibiting her from visiting her parental home. (²)

4. On account of his change of religion. (³)

5. On account of his notorious dissoluteness of morals. (⁴)

6. On account of wasting his property and refusing to support her. (⁵)

7. On account of having committed a crime, compelling him to flee from the country. (⁶)

8. On account of his physical impotence, if admitted by

(¹) Kethuboth, p. 75; Eben Ha-Ezer CLIV. 1.

(²) Eben Ha-Ezer CLIV. 3, gloss; compare, also, LXXIV. 1-8. In the gloss just referred to, wife-beating is decried as a shameful, un-Jewish treatment. An interesting Law Report of the thirteenth century concerning a case in which a Jewish husband was accused of such ill treatment toward his wife, is found in the Responses of Nachmanides. (Teshuboth Ramban, No. 102.) See the *American Israelite*, Vol. XXX., No. 51, p. 4.

(³) Eben Ha-Ezer CLIV. 3, gloss, and Beth Joseph, ch. CXXXIV.

(⁴) Eben Ha-Ezer *ibid.*, § 1, gloss.

(⁵) Eben Ha-Ezer *ibid.*, § 3.

(⁶) Eben Ha-Ezer *ibid.*, § 9.

him; and, according to some authorities, also on account of his persistent refusal of matrimonial intercourse. (¹)

d. DIVORCE ENFORCED BY COURT AGAINST THE WILL OF BOTH PARTIES.

§ 74.

Under Jewish jurisdiction such a divorce, without the application and desire of either of the parties, was formerly enforced in the following cases:

1. Where a marriage had been contracted which, though formally binding, was regarded voidable on account of being against a Biblical or Rabbinical Law prohibiting such a marriage. (²)

For instance, if a man remarried his divorced wife after her second marriage; or if he married within those degrees prohibited only by the Talmudic extensions, as his maternal uncle's widow. (³)

This, however, did not apply to the incestuous and adulterous marriages (עריות) expressly prohibited in the eighteenth chapter of Leviticus, as these were regarded as a nullity, requiring no formal divorce. (⁴)

2. Where the husband was willing to continue his marriage, though the wife had been found guilty of wilful adultery. (⁵)

It must be remembered that, according to the view of

(¹) Eben Ha-Ezer CLIV. 7, gloss; compare, also, LXXVII. 1.
(²) Talm. Kethuboth, p. 77; Eben Ha-Ezer CLIV. 20.
(³) See above, p. 38.
(⁴) See above, p. 33 *sq*.
(⁵) Eben Ha-Ezer XI. 1; CXV. 8.

the Jewish Law, adultery is regarded not merely as misconduct and private injury, which may be condoned by the offended party, but as a crime which invalidates the moral foundation of marriage, so as to make its continuation absolutely impossible. ([1])

3. Where sanitary considerations did not permit the conjugal cohabitation, as, if one of the parties became affected with the incurable disease of leprosy. Divorce was, however, not enforced in such a case where the other party consented to continue marriage without cohabitation. ([2])

4. According to the view that procreation is one of the principal ends of marriage, divorce was anciently enforced also in the case of a marriage which, after existing ten years, had proved to be childless. Later authorities, however, disapproved the enforcement of a divorce in this case. ([3])

6. *CAUSES FOR DIVORCE CONSIDERED IN MODERN LEGISLATION.*

§ 75.

The provisions of the Rabbinical Code concerning the causes of divorce, as just set forth, are in many respects at variance with those of modern legislation. Several of the causes defined in the former code are not regarded sufficient in modern law; while, on the other hand, the latter grants divorce for some causes not recognized in

---

([1]) Compare above, p. 27.
([2]) Eben Ha-Ezer CLIV. 1.
([3]) Eben Ha-Ezer *ibid.*, § 10 and gloss.

the Rabbinical Law. The laws of the different countries on this subject are far from being uniform. (¹)

We shall confine ourselves to a few short statements concerning the laws of England and of the United States.

Until recently, the doctrine of the law of England was that of the Roman Church, which regards marriage as indissoluble. All matters of marriage belonged to the jurisdiction of the ecclesiastical courts, and these were in the habit of granting divorces only *a mensa et thoro*, for various causes, especially for adultery and cruelty. In certain cases, *e. g.*, where the parties were within the prohibited degrees of consanguinity and affinity, these courts declared the marriage null and void. But they had no power to dissolve a marriage valid and binding in its origin, for causes arising subsequent to its solemnization. For that purpose recourse had to be had to Parliament. The Divorce Act of 1858 abolished the jurisdiction of the ecclesiastical courts, and constituted a new court for divorces and matrimonial causes. This court may grant divorce for the cause of the wife's adultery, and for certain grosser forms of this crime on the husband's part, and judicial separation is the remedy for certain other causes.

In this country, each State of the Union determines the causes for which divorce may be granted. Thus, the provisions being different in the different States, it is very difficult to make a general statement of the law. In South Carolina a divorce is not allowed for any cause; in New York, only for adultery; but in most of the States

---

(¹) A condensed synopsis of these different laws of modern civilized countries is found in WOOLSEY's Divorce and Divorce Legislation, second edition, Chapters IV. and V.

it is allowed for several causes. The principal of the causes are the following: (¹)

1. ADULTERY.

2. CRUELTY, differently described in the laws of the different States, as: intolerable severity, injurious treatment, indignities making life burdensome, etc.

3. DESERTION, also termed abandonment, absence without good cause. The time of willful absence required to constitute desertion is differently fixed in the statutes, varying from one to five years.

4. HABITUAL DRUNKENNESS.

5. IMPRISONMENT FOR CRIME. The time of imprisonment varies in different States.

6. NEGLECT TO PROVIDE FOR THE WIFE'S MAINTENANCE AND SUPPORT, though being able to do so. Also GROSS NEGLECT OF DUTY on the part of the wife is ground of divorce in some of the States.

7. IMPOTENCE — in several States qualified as existing before marriage, and in this case even a cause for ANNULLING THE MARRIAGE, so as to render it void *ab initio*.

8. Joining a religious society which holds marriage to be unlawful is by the statutes of a few States made a ground for divorce.

9. In some of the States the causes for which divorce may be granted are wholly or in part left to the discretion of the courts.

---

(1) See BISHOP's Marriage and Divorce, I., Books VI. and VII., and WOOLSEY's Divorce and Divorce Legislation, Chap. V.

7. THE BILL OF DIVORCE.

§ 76.

To constitute a valid divorce, according to the Jewish Law, a written document of divorce must be delivered by the husband to the wife, either in person or through an appointed agent. This document (*Sepher Kerithoth*—"Bill of Divorce," as called in the Bible, or *Get*—simply "Document," as termed by the rabbis) is to be signed by two competent witnesses, and the delivery must also take place in the presence of two witnesses. Later custom required the presence of at least ten persons in order to give the act more publicity. It appears that up to the time of the compilation of the Mishnah the form of this document was not yet strictly fixed, it only having been required to contain, besides the date and the names of the parties, the words, "Thou art now free for any man." [1]

Although the document may be written in any language, it has become customary to use exclusively the rabbinical idiom, which is a mixture of Hebrew and Aramaic. The present form of the document was probably established by the Babylonian teachers of the fourth century, who also laid down some very minute rules for its somewhat peculiar orthography and caligraphy. [2] Later authorities still increased these rules and surrounded the act of writing and delivering the document with numerous formalities, which by no means have a religious but merely a juridical character. In order to secure a prompt execution of these minute rules and formalities, it is

---

[1] See Mishna Gittin IX. 3.
[2] See Talm. Gittin, p. 85b.

required that the act be conducted and supervised by a rabbi or an authorized man well versed in the law. (³)

8. FORM OF THE BILL OF DIVORCE.

§ 77.

The following is a translation of the form of that document:

"On the (5th) day of the week, the (20th) day of the month (Ab), in the year (5643) of the creation of the world, according to the number we reckon here, ———, the city which is situated on the river ———, and contains wells for water, I, ———, son of ———, who stand this day in ———, the city situated on the river ———, and containing wells of water, do hereby consent, with my own will, without force, free and unrestrained, to grant a Bill of Divorce to thee, my wife ———, daughter of ———, who hast been my wife from time past, and with this I free, release and divorce thee, that thou mayest have control and power over thyself, from now and hereafter, to be married to any man whom thou mayest choose, and no man shall hinder thee from this day forever more, and thus thou art free for every man. And this shall be unto thee from me a Bill of Divorce, a letter of freedom, and a document of dismission according to the Law of Moses and Israel.

"———, son of ———, witness.
"———, son of ———, witness."

(³) The particulars concerning the act of writing and delivering the bill of divorce are treated of in Eben Ha-Ezer, Chapter CXX.-CLIII., and in the *Seder ha-get* which follows chapter CLIV. A lucid abstract thereof in German is found in Dr. J. Hamburger's *Real-Encyclopædie fuer Bibel und Talmud*, II., pp. 1082-1087.

CHAPTER XVI.

THE JEWISH LAW OF DIVORCE IN MODERN TIMES.

a. A MODERN QUESTION AND ITS ATTEMPTED SOLUTION.

§ 78.

As long as the Jews had autonomy in all their matrimonial affairs, and Jewish courts were permitted to exercise a kind of ecclesiastical jurisdiction in cases of divorce, they were strictly governed by the Rabbinical Law concerning such matters.

Since the beginning of the present century this autonomy has ceased in most of the European countries. Here, in America, it never existed. Under these circumstances, a valid marriage can be dissolved by the competent courts of the State only. The laws by which these courts are governed differ in many respects from the rules of the Rabbinical Code. The rabbi in our time has no power or authority to enforce a dissolution of marriage, where it is required by the Jewish law, or to conduct the act of a ritual *Get*, so long as the marriage has not been duly dissolved by the competent court of the country.

In general, the Jewish parties whose marriage has been dissolved by court apply for a ritual *Get*, in order to be permitted to remarry according to the Jewish Law; and in this case the rabbi will comply with their request. But is the act of giving a ritual *Get* to be performed in our time according to the minute rules and numerous formalities which have been established by the rabbis of ancient times? And how shall the case be treated where one of the parties whose marriage has been dissolved by a judicial decision refuses to submit to the formality of a ritual *Get?* Is, then, the other party forever debarred from contracting a new marriage?

These questions have engaged the attention of modern rabbis who have treated of this subject in pamphlets and discussed it also in various conferences. The late Dr. S. HOLDHEIM, in his *Autonomie der Rabbinen* (1843) comes to the conclusion that divorce, being, according to the Jewish law, a civil act only, is to be entirely submitted to the laws of the country, and a judicial decision of the competent authorities declaring a marriage dissolved makes the ritual *Get* entirely superfluous. This view, though forcibly contradicted by other learned rabbis, [1] is at present more and more gaining ground among the followers of Reformed Judaism.

At the first Jewish Synod of Leipzig (1869) and the second of Augsburg (1871) motions were brought in by the Rabbis Dr. GEIGER, Dr. WECHSLER, and others, to the effect that the forms of the ritual *Get* are to be modified, that the Aramaic language of that document is to be replaced by the vernacular, and that in the case where a Jewish marriage has been dissolved by the decision of competent courts, and the husband refuses to submit to

---

[1] Especially by the late Dr. Z. FRANKEL, in his *Zeitschrift*, vol. I.

the act of the Jewish *Get*, the wife shall be permitted to remarry without such a document.

These motions were referred to a committee for report in the expected third Synod, which, however, has not yet been convened.

b. PROPOSITION SUBMITTED TO THE PHILADELPHIA CONFERENCE.

§ 79.

More decided was the Rabbinical Conference of Philadelphia (1869); it entirely indorsed the views which HOLDHEIM had advanced. Among other propositions submitted to this Conference by the late Rev. Dr. EINHORN was also one regarding Divorce. It reads substantially as follows:

"The ESSENTIALLY civil character of the Jewish form of concluding marriage and of divorce has been settled beyond question by theological researches, [1] and the highly important consequences resulting from the two acts conflict with this character just as little as, for instance, the religious prohibition of theft conflicts with the nature of purchase or heritage, by which property is acquired, and which certainly belongs to the forum of civil law. The marriage relation in itself is, indeed, even from the standpoint of reform, a RELIGIOUS institution, and so is certainly also the entrance into that relation a RELIGIOUS act; this view, however, can not deprive the MEANS BY WHICH SUCH A RELATION IS ENTERED UPON—the forms of acquiring a certain person for such a union—of their civil character; and the Bible nowhere speaks of any religious forms with reference to the act of concluding marriage. But the religious consecration of marriage, an institution to which religion attaches such high importance, could not and should not be omitted. Divorce still more clearly appears as a civil

---

[1] Especially HOLDHEIM's *Autonomie der Rabbinen*.

act, recognized only, if not merely TOLERATED by religion. The Bible does not mention the BILL OF DIVORCE (Deut. xxiv. 1) as a subject of POSITIVE COMMAND, but only incidentally as a written instrument which the husband has to execute and to deliver to the wife he intends to dismiss; and though it PRESUPPOSES an immorality in the woman (*Ervath dabar*) as the cause of dismissing, it by no means commands the dismissal, and confines itself only to prohibiting the remarrying of the divorced woman after she had contracted another marriage which again had been dissolved. Rabbinical Judaism also, though in various cases considering divorce a religious duty, could not remove the civil character of divorce and introduce a religious form for that act. It prescribes no benedictions for it, as it does for the act of concluding marriage. The concluding words of the bill of divorce (דת משה וישראל —'According to the Law of Moses and Israel'), the high antiquity of which is by no means established beyond doubt, confer in nowise a religious character on the act, as indeed some authorities maintain that these very words were anciently in use also in other Jewish documents which had no religious character at all. (¹) According to the opinion of R. SIMON, a bill of divorce executed by a non-Jewish court has full force. (Gittin, 10*b*) And how could religion, if not raising its voice in protest, assume in this matter any other but a passive position? Where two persons unite in community for life, it is the function of religion to offer consecration, sanctification and blessing, as God consecrated and blessed the covenant of the first couple. But if the holy bonds are severed, religion can only tolerate the act in sorrow and silence; it may offer consolation to the innocent sufferer or rebuke the conscience of the guilty, but certainly can not invest the act with its consecration. Religious forms of divorce are without root in the soil of our history, and can but be artificial. I therefore do not believe that it is the intention of this Conference to create a religious consecration where none ever existed and where there is nothing to consecrate.

---

(1) Compare Maimonides' and Heller's Commentary to Mishna Jadayim IV. 8; Tosephoth to Baba Bathra, p. 162*a*, s. v. לפי, and Nissim to Gittin, 10*b*, and Mishna Gittin, 85*b*.

"But it may appear to us as an imperious duty to recognize, IN THE NAME OF RELIGION, the dissolution of Jewish marriages, which, according to the Rabbinical Code, is effected, without a judicial process, by the parties themselves, under the supervision and direction of an expert scholar (*chacham*), as an act exclusively belonging to the function of the judicial authorities of the State, and to declare the so-called ritual *Get*, in all cases, as of no effect.

"It is different, however, with the GROUNDS OF DIVORCE. On this point Judaism must reserve to itself the examination of the provisions of the State laws. Before the forum of the law of God, which regards husband and wife as one person, divorce can be justified only on the grounds of an actual disturbance of the moral basis of conjugal life, as, for instance, by conjugal infidelity, criminal abandonment of home, and the like, whether on the part of the husband or the wife. As, according to our religious views, some of the provisions of the Rabbinical Code must be rejected, for instance, those which regard childlessness or certain loathsome diseases, or even the engagement in a disgusting trade, as sufficient grounds for divorce * * * * ; so the State law may sometimes decree the divorce on grounds which are insufficient to religion, and the latter may be forced to record its veto against the dissolution of the holy covenant. In questions involving one of the most important institutions, religion must not unconditionally and blindly submit to the State law, and would, in refusing its sanction, when requested to remarry people thus divorced, only protect its good right without trespassing upon the sphere of the State. Such a conflict were, of course, to be regretted; but it must not be forgotten that its anticipation will in many cases prevent the desire for obtaining a judicial divorce. * * * *

"It may, however, be appropriate for the rabbi, in such cases, after a close examination of the contents of the judicial document of divorce, and after having approved of the causes as religiously sufficient, to certify to the fact, with the concurrence of some of his colleagues." ([1])

([1]) Protokolle, p. 56–58.

C. RESOLUTIONS PASSED BY THAT CONFERENCE.

§ 80.

This proposition was elaborately discussed in the Conference, which, in general, agreed with the views expressed therein. Two dissenting members ([1]) made a motion to the effect that the ritual *Get* should not be entirely abolished, but only modified according to the views and circumstances of our time, in the way as proposed by the progressive rabbis in Germany. But the motion was lost. The same was the case with the motion from another side, ([2]) to strike out that passage which reserves to the rabbi the right to examine the grounds of a divorce decreed by the civil courts. Finally, the following resolution ([3]) was passed, which essentially embodies the views expressed in the submitted proposition:

"The dissolution of marriage is, on Mosaic and Rabbinical grounds, a civil act only, which never received religious consecration. It is to be recognized, therefore, as an act emanating altogether from the judicial authorities of the State. The so-called ritual *Get* is in all cases declared null and void.

"The dissolution of marriage, pronounced by a civil court, is also fully valid in the eyes of Judaism, if it can be ascertained from the judicial documents that both parties consented to the divorce; where, however, the court issues a decree against one or the other party, by constraint, Judaism recognizes the validity of the divorce then only, if the cause assigned is sufficient in conformity with the spirit of the Jewish religion. It is recommended, however, that the officiating rabbi, in rendering a decision, obtain the concurrence of competent colleagues." ([4])

([1]) The Rev. Drs. SONNESCHEIN and MIELZINER.
([2]) The Rev. Drs. S. HIRSCH and CHRONIK.
([3]) On motion of the Rev. Dr. S. ADLER.
([4]) Protokolle, p. 26–36.

d. EXPLANATORY REMARKS TO THE RESOLUTIONS PASSED.

§ 81.

One or two points in the above resolution may here be further explained. In declaring that "the dissolution of marriage, pronounced by a civil court, is also fully valid in the eyes of Judaism, if it can be ascertained from the judicial documents that BOTH PARTIES CONSENTED TO THE DIVORCE," the resolution does not refer to a MUTUAL AGREEMENT of the parties to be divorced, but to a final CONSENT on both sides, in a case where one of the parties, on some complaint, petitions for a divorce, and the other party, without contesting the allegations, is willing to accept the divorce; for mutual consent of the parties, without proved complaints from either side, is, by the laws in the United States, not sufficient for divorce. ([1])

Regarding the reservation made in this resolution, that the rabbi, before remarrying a divorced party, is to examine the causes for which the judicial divorce has been granted, it appears from the proceedings of the Conference that such a reservation was necessary in view of the great laxity in granting divorces which notoriously exists in some parts of this country, especially in Territories and States where, in addition to the specified causes, a general discriminating power is vested in the courts. There it not rarely occurs that a judicial divorce is obtained by one of the parties on very loose grounds, and sometimes even without the knowledge of the other party. In such cases it is certainly the duty of the rabbi to refrain from giving religious sanction to a second marriage, where the former one was so frivolously dissolved.

([1]) See Protokolle, p. 36, note; compare, also, above, p. 127, note.

e. CONCLUSION.

§ 82.

In conclusion, we must repeat here what has already been stated above, in the chapter on the SOURCES OF THE JEWISH MARRIAGE LAW, that the resolutions and decisions of modern Rabbinical Conferences and Synods have not yet been generally accepted as authoritative by the Jewish community. Even many of the progressive rabbis, both in this country and abroad, have yet some hesitation in acting upon them in their official capacity, so long as these resolutions have not been indorsed by a general Synod, to be convoked by a majority of the congregations. The strictly conservative rabbi, who regards the dicta of the Shulchan Aruch as the ever-binding law in Israel, will, of course, not yield even to the authority of such a Synod, and consequently refuse to sanction a second marriage of a woman who has been divorced by a judicial decree without having obtained a ritual *Get* from the former husband.

[THE END]

INDEX.

A.

	PAGE.
AARONITES or *Cohanim*, meaning of,	59
Special Prohibitions concerning the Marriage of,	59
Resolutions passed regarding the Prohibitions,	59, 60
ABANDONMENT, Ground of Divorce, in Modern Laws,	127
ABBA AREKA, Protesting against giving Minor Daughters in Marriage,	73
ABSENT AND NOT HEARD OF,	112
ADULTERY, treated in the Mosaic Law as a Capital Crime,	20
The Wife's, can not be condoned, but necessitates a Divorce,	27, 124
Persons guilty of, not permitted to marry the Partner of their Crime,	42
Strong Suspicion of, Cause for Divorce,	122
Ground of Divorce in Modern Legislation,	127
AFFINITY. See *Consanguinity*.	
AGE, Legal, for Contracting Marriage,	71 and note.
AGENT, Betrothal through, formerly admitted,	80
Bill of Divorce delivered by,	128
AGREEMENT, of Parties, sufficient for Divorce, according to Jewish, but not according to the Laws in the United States,	121 and note.
ARUSIN, one of the Rabbinical Terms for Betrothment,	76
AUB on Intermarriage,	50
AUNT, Marriage of Nephew with, prohibited,	35, 38, 39
AUTHORITY of the Modern Rabbi in regard to Marriage and Divorce defined,	22, 84, 94, 130
AUTONOMY, Jewish, in all Matrimonial Affairs, ceased in Modern times,	22, 93, 130

B.

	PAGE.
BALDACHIN. See *Chuppa.*	
BARRENNESS, Whether a Ground of Divorce,	125
BE-AH, Term for a certain Primitive Mode of contracting Marriage,	78, note.
BENARY, *De Hebræorum Levirata,*	note, 55
BENEDICTION of Betrothal,	82
Of Nuptials,	84, 85, 90, 93
BERCHATH ARUSIN, meaning Benediction of Betrothal,	82
BERCHOTH NISSU-IN, meaning Benedictions of Nuptials,	84
BETROTHMENT, Its Nature in the Rabbinical Law different from that in Modern Law,	76
How effected,	77sq.
Former Interval between Betrothal and Nuptials,	82
Combination of both Acts,	85, 90
BILL OF DIVORCE, Rabbinical Rules concerning,	125
Form of,	129
Resolutions of the Philadelphia Conference concerning,	135
BISHOP on Marriage and Divorce, 8, 26, 34, 37, 68, 73, 100, 111, 121, 127	
BROTHER'S WIFE, Marriage with, prohibited,	35
Former Exception in Case of Levirate,	55

C.

CAUSES OF DIVORCE, By the Jewish Law,	121–124
Considered in Modern Laws,	125–127
CHALITZA, Meaning of,	55
Biblical Precept,	56
Modern View of,	57
Resolutions passed concerning,	58
CHANGE OF RELIGION, A Cause for Divorce,	122, 123
CHILDREN, Religious Status of, in Mixed Marriages,	97
CHUPPA, Meaning of,	83
Representation of,	85
Not generally used in Our Time,	90
CIVIL MARRIAGE,	93
Synodical Resolutions concerning,	94
CODE of the Rabbinical Marriage Laws, when and by whom established,	22
Modifications of its Provisions in Modern Times,	23
COHABITATION,	99, 101, 122, 124, 125
COMBINATION of Betrothal and Nuptials,	85
CONDITIONAL CONSENT,	67, 68

INDEX.

CONDONATION of Wife's Proved Adultery not admitted in the Jewish Law, - 27, 124
CONFERENCES, Rabbinical, modifying some Laws of the Jewish Marriage Code, - 23
    Their Resolutions not generally accepted, - 24, 137
CONJUGAL RIGHTS AND DUTIES, - 98–104
CONSANGUINITY AND AFFINITY. Ch. V, - 33
    Prohibitions of, based on Morality; hence binding upon all Nations, - 35
    Biblical Degrees of, - 35
    Their classification, - 41
    Different Reasons for the Prohibitions, - 36
    Talmudical Extensions, - 37, 38, 41
    The Guiding Principle of the Extensions, - 37, note.
    Marriages within the Biblical Degrees void; within the Talmudical, voidable, - 33
CONSENT OF PARTIES:
    Essential in contracting Marriage, - 66
    But mere consent not sufficient; it must be accompanied by a certain legally established act, - 77
CONSENT OF PARENTS, whether required for Marriage, - 69
CONSEQUENCES of a Premature Remarriage, - 111
CONTRACT OF MARRIAGE, differs from other Contracts, - 24, 25
COUSINS, Marriage between, permitted, but in Ohio unlawful, - 40 and note.
CRIME, Committance of, as Ground of Divorce in the Jewish Law, 123
    In Modern Law, - 127
CRUELTY, as Ground of Divorce, in the Jewish Law, - 123
    In Modern Law, - 127
CUP OF WINE, Custom of, at the Marriage Ceremony, - 85, 93

D.

DEAF AND DUMB, the Marriage of, - 70, 71 and note.
DEATH, Dissolving Marriage, - 108
    Evidence of, - 109–114
DECEASED WIFE'S SISTER, Marriage with, permitted, - 39
    Where not permitted, - 39, note 1
DEGREES:
    Within which Marriage Prohibited, - 33–38
    Biblical, - 34–36
    Talmudical Extensions of, - 37, 38
    Not Objectionable Degrees, - 39, 40
    Table of Prohibited, - 41

	PAGE.
DESERTION. See *Abandonment*.	
DISEASES, Certain, as Ground of Divorce,	122, 123
DISGUSTING TRADE as Ground of Divorce,	123
DISREGARD of Ritual Laws,	81, 122
DISSOLUTENESS of Morals a Cause for Divorce,	123
DISSOLUTION of Marriage,	108
DIVORCE, Ethical View of,	115
Necessarily admitted by Law,	116
Mosaic Regulations,	116
Rabbinical Provisions to prevent Inconsiderate Divorces,	119
Restriction of the Right of,	120
Different Kinds of,	120
Causes of, in the Jewish Law,	121–124
Modern Legislation concerning,	125–127
Bill of,	128, 129
The Jewish Law of, in Modern Times,	130–137
DIVORCED WOMAN, When prohibited to be remarried to her Former Husband,	42
Lapse of Time required before contracting a New Marriage,	61, 62
DOTAL PROPERTY,	104, 105
DOUBTFUL BETROTHMENT,	81
DOWRY,	30, 86, 120, 121
Forfeiture of,	120
DUSCHAK on the Mosaic-Talmudic Marriage Law,	7, note.
On Marriage of the Deaf and Dumb,	71, note.

E.

EBEN HA-EZER, Name of the Rabbinical Code of Marriage Laws,	22
EINHORN on Intermarriage,	51
Ritual of Wedding Ceremony,	93, note.
On Divorce,	132–134
ENGAGEMENT,	77
ERROR AND FALSE REPRESENTATION, Whether affecting the Marriage Contract,	69
ETHICAL DOCTRINES, Distinction between, and LAW,	13
ETHICAL VIEW OF MARRIAGE,	15*sq*.
Of Divorce,	115
EVIDENCE OF DEATH, Rabbinical Rules concerning,	109–112
Resolutions of Modern Rabbis concerning,	113, 114
EXTENSIONS, Rabbinical, of the Prohibited Degrees,	37, 38

F.

	PAGE
FALSE REPRESENTATION, whether affecting the Marriage Contract,	69
FORCE, Consent obtained by,	66
FORM OF MARRIAGE, not fixed in the Mosaic Law,	20
But established in the Talmudic Law,	21, 75
In Ancient Times, Chap. X.	75–89
In Modern Time, Chap. XI.	90–93
FORM OF KETHUBA,	87
FORM OF THE BILL OF DIVORCE,	129
FORMULA of Betrothment,	78, 79
Of the Wedding Ceremony,	92
FRANKEL, Z., *Grundlinien des mosaisch-talmudischen Eherechts*,	7, 26 (note), 73, 79, 95, 109, 113, 121

G.

GAONIM (title of the Highest Authorities after the Close of the Talmud) modifying some Provisions of the Talmudic Law,	21
GEIGER, on Reforms needed in the Jewish Marriage Law,	23, note.
On Intermarriage,	50
On *Chalitza*,	58, note.
On the Ritual *Get*,	131
GERSCHOM, Celebrated Rabbi (eleventh century) interdicted Polygamy,	30
Restricted the Husband's Right of Divorce,	120
GERUSHIN, name of Maimonides' Treatise on Divorce,	21
GET, the Talmudic Term for the Bill of Divorce,	128
GITTIN, name of the Talmudic Treatise on Divorce,	20, note.
GUTMANN, on Levirate Marriage,	23, note.

H.

HABITUAL DRUNKENNESS, a Cause for Divorce in Modern Legislation,	127
HAMBURGER, Talm. Encyclopædia,	128, note.
HIRSCH, S., on Intermarriage,	52, note.
HOCHMUTH, on Marriage of the Deaf and Dumb,	71, note.
HOLDHEIM, on Reform of the Jewish Marriage Law,	23, note.
On Intermarriage,	52, note.
On Divorce,	131
HUEBSCH, on Intermarriage,	97, note.
Wedding Ritual,	93, note.
HUSBAND AND WIFE,	96–107
Husband's Duties,	98–101
His Rights,	102

I.

	PAGE.
IDENTIFICATION, Rabbinical Rules concerning,	112
IDIOTS, incompetent to contract Marriage,	70
ILL TREATMENT, as Ground of Divorce,	123, 127
ILLEGITIMACY, not regarded in Hereditary Succession,	95

IMPEDIMENTS TO MARRIAGE. See *Prohibited Marriages*, and *Qualifications to contract Marriage*.

IMPOTENCE, a Ground of Divorce in the Jewish Law,	123
In Modern Laws,	127
INCESTUOUS MARRIAGES, are null and void from the beginning,	33, 124
INFANT MARRIAGES in Former Times,	72–74
*INSANE PERSONS, incompetent to contract Marriage,	70
INSULTS, as Ground of Divorce,	122
INTERMARRIAGE, or Mixed Marriages:	
Biblical Prohibition to intermarry with Certain Nations,	45
The Assigned Reason applicable also to Other Nations; hence the Rabbinical Extension of the Prohibition to Gentiles in General,	46
Christian Emperors interdicting Intermarriage with Jews under Penalty of Death,	46
The Question of Intermarriage submitted to the French Sanhedrin by Napoleon I.; Evading Answer of the Sanhedrin,	47
The Question before the Braunschweig Rabbinical Conference,	48
The Decision not indorsed by the Augsburg Synod,	ibid., note.
Weighty Reasons against Intermarriage,	49
Opinions on the Subject:	
Philippson's,	48
Geiger's,	50
Aub's,	50
Einhorn's,	51
Wise's,	52–54
INTERVAL between the Act of Betrothal and Nuptials in Former Times,	82
INTOXICATION, when invalidating the Marriage Contract,	70
ISHUTH, Name of Maimonides, Treatise on Marriage,	21
ISSERLES, Rabbi Moses, Glossator to the Rabbinical Code of Marriage Laws,	22

J.

JASTROW and SZOLD, Wedding Ritual,	93, note.
JURISDICTION of Jewish Courts in Matrimonial Affairs abolished in Modern Times,	22, 130

K.

	PAGE.
KALISCH, M., on Marriage,	7, 26 (note), 39
KARO, Rabbi Joseph, author of the Rabbinical Code,	21
KASEPH, meaning a Piece of Money, one of the Former Means of contracting Marriage,	78
In Later Times, replaced by the Wedding Ring,	79
KETHUBA, Meaning and Purpose of,	85, 86
Form of,	87
Former Importance of,	88
Why unnecessary in Our Time,	89
KETHUBOTH, Name of the Talmudic Treatise on Dower and Marriage Settlements,	20, note.
KIDDUSHIN, Term for Betrothal or the Act of contracting Marriage,	27, 76
Name of one of the Talmudic Treatises on Marriage,	20, note.
KOHEN, or COHEN, meaning a Descendant of the Priestly Tribe, identical with *Aaronite*,	59, 96

L.

LANDSBERGER, on the Custom of abstaining from celebrating Marriage between Pasach and Shabuoth,	64, note.
LAW, Distinction between, and Ethical Doctrine,	13
Sources of the Jewish Law of Marriage,	20-22
LEGAL VIEW OF MARRIAGE,	25
LEVIRATE, meaning of,	55
LEVITICAL DEGREES, meaning of,	36
LOEW, Leopold, *Eherechtliche Studien*,	7, 26 (note), 79, 80
LUCID INTERVALS, Marriage contracted in, valid.	70
LUNACY, an Impediment to Marriage,	70

M.

MAIMONIDES, Rabbi Moses, author of a Code of the Talmudic Laws,	21
MAMZER, Meaning of the Term,	43
Prohibition concerning,	43, 44
The Offspring of,	96
MARITAL DUTIES AND RIGHTS,	98-104
MARRIAGE, its Importance and Sacredness,	13
Ethical View of,	15
Legal View of,	25
Is more than a mere Civil Contract,	26
Prohibitions concerning,	33
When void and when voidable,	33, 124
Qualifications to contract,	66

146   INDEX.

	PAGE.
Form of concluding,	75
Consummation of,	83
Modern Mode of solemnizing,	90
Jewish Marriage placed under the Authority of the Laws of the Country,	94
Civil Marriage,	93, 94
Dissolution of,	108
MARRIAGE SETTLEMENTS,	86, 88, 89
MENTAL CAPACITY, an Essential Requirement for contracting Marriage,	66, 70
ME-UN, meaning of the Term,	72
MINOR, when regarded as,	71
Marriage contracted by, void,	71
MINOR DAUGHTER, Exception formerly made in favor of,	72–74
MIXED MARRIAGE. See *Intermarriage*.	
Religious Status of Children in a,	97
MODERN Mode of Solemnizing Marriage,	90–93
MODIFICATION of the Jewish Law of Marriage and Divorce,	22–24
MONOGAMY AND POLYGAMY, Ch. IV.	28–32
See *Polygamy*.	
MOURNING, a Temporary Impediment,	63

N.

NECHSE MELUG, Meaning of,	105
NEDUNJA, meaning Dotal Property,	104
NEPHEW, prohibited to marry his Aunt,	35, 38
NIECE permitted to marry her Uncle,	39
NISSU-IN, Hebrew Term for Nuptials,	83
NOT OBJECTIONABLE DEGREES,	39, 40
NUPTIALS, Essential Ceremonies of,	83
Religious Ceremonies of,	84
The Joint Act of Betrothal and Nuptials,	85
Ceremonies of, in Modern Times,	90–93

O.

OBSTRUCTIVE DAYS for celebrating Marriage,	63–65
OFFSPRING of Lawful and Unlawful Marriages,	95–97

P.

PARAPHERNAL PROPERTY, meaning of,	104
PERMITTED DEGREES,	39, 40
PHILIPPSON, Dr. Ludwig, on Intermarriage,	48
On the Principle underlying the Prohibited Degrees,	39, note.

	PAGE.
POLYGAMY, contravening the Will of God and the Design of Marriage,	16
Prevailing among all Oriental Nations, it was tolerated by the Mosaic and the Talmudic Laws, but restricted and never very common among Israelites,	28–30
Was regarded as Incompatible with Domestic Peace and Happiness,	29, note.
Expressly interdicted by a Rabbinical Synod under Rabbi Gershom, in the eleventh century,	30
Resolutions passed by the Philadelphia Rabbinical Conference concerning Polygamy,	31
Not directly condemned in the New Testament, but prohibited by the Laws of Justinian, and since regarded by all Civilized Nations as a Punishable Crime,	32
PREGNANCY, a Temporary Impediment to Marriage,	62
PRIOR MARRIAGE, undissolved, how affecting a New Marriage Contract,	31, 111 and note.
PROHIBITED MARRIAGES,	33–60
PROHIBITED DEGREES. See *Degrees*.	
PROPERTY, Wife's,	104–107
PUBERTY, Age of, when assumed in the Jewish Law,	71
In the Common Law,	*Ibid.*, note.

Q.

QUALIFICATIONS required to contract Marriage,	66
Of Witnesses,	81

R.

RABBI. See *Authority*.

RABBINICAL CONFERENCES, modifying the Jewish Marriage Law,	23
REFUSAL of Connubial Rights, as Ground of Divorce,	122, 124
To follow to another Domicil,	122
To maintain the Wife, as Ground of Divorce,	123, 127
RESOLUTIONS, passed by the:	
Braunschweig Rabbinical Conference,	48
Jewish Synod of Augsburg,	58, 60, 62, 65, 81, 92, 94, 114
Philadelphia Conference,	31, 58, 59, 92, 113, 135

S.

SAALSCHUETZ, Mos. Recht.,	7, 117
SABBATH AND FESTIVALS, Marriage not permitted to be contracted on,	63
SANHEDRIN, French, Declaration of, concerning Intermarriage,	47

	PAGE.
SANITARY CONSIDERATIONS, Divorce on account of,	125
SHAMMAI AND HILLEL, Schools of, differing in the Interpretation of the Mosaic Law concerning the Causes of Divorce,	119
SHIDDUCHIN, Rabbinical Term for Engagement,	77
SH'TAR, meaning a Writing,	78
One of the Former Means of contracting Marriage,	79
SHULCHAN ARUCH, General Name of R. Joseph Karo's Code of Rabbinical Laws,	21
SOLEMNIZATION OF MARRIAGE in Modern Time,	90–93
SOPHERIM (the Scribes), enacting New Regulations of the Marriage Law,	21
Extending the Prohibited Degrees,	33, 37
SPADONES, Prohibition concerning,	44
STEP BROTHER AND STEP-SISTER, Marriage between, whether permitted,	40
SUCKLING CHILD, a Temporary Impediment to the Mother's Marriage,	62
Synodical Resolutions concerning this Impediment,	62
SUSPICION, Impediments to Marriage on account of,	43
SYNODS, Modern, modifying some Provisions of the Jewish Marriage Law,	23

T.—V.

TABLE OF PROHIBITED DEGREES,	41
TEMPORARY IMPEDIMENTS,	61
TEKANOTH SHUM,	107
TZON BARZEL, meaning of,	105
UNCLE and NIECE, marriage of, permitted,	39
VIOLATION OF MORAL DECENCY, as Ground of Divorce,	122
VOID and VOIDABLE, Distinction between, regarding Marriage,	33, 34 and note, 66, 124

W—Y.

WECHSLER, B., on the Formalities of the Act of Divorce,	23, note.
WEDDING RING, Origin of,	79 and note.
Symbolical Meaning of,	80 and note.
One or two Wedding Rings,	91
Resolutions concerning,	92
WIDOW, Lapse of Time required before her remarriage,	61, 62
WIDOWER, Lapse of Time required before his remarriage,	63
WIFE's Duties and Rights,	103
Property,	104–107

	PAGE.
WISE, I. M., on Intermarriage,	52
On *Chalitza*,	58
WITNESSES to Marriage essential for its validity,	81
To Death,	110
To Divorce,	128
WOOLSEY, on Divorce Legislation,	126, 127
YABAM (Brother-in-law),	55
YEBAMOTH, Name of the Talmudic Treatise on the Levirate,	20, note.
YIBBUM, Rabbinical Term for Levirate,	55
Name of one Part of Maimonides' Code treating of Levirate,	21

THE AMERICAN HEBREW PUBLISHING HOUSE.

Any of the following publications will be sent postpaid to any address on receipt of affixed price.

FAMILY BIBLE.
    English only. Translated by the late Rev. Isaac Leeser, from the Massoretic Hebrew text, on the basis of the English version. The only correct English translation. BOUND in SHEEP, 18mo........................ $1 50

INFLUENCE OF JUDAISM on the Protestant Reformation.
    By Dr. H. Graetz.................... 50

THE SEMITIC NATION.
    By Dr. D. Chwolson, Ord. Prof. at the Imp. University of St. Petersburg.............................. 50

A SERIES OF LETTERS on the Evidences of Christianity.
    By Benjamin Dias Fernandez.................. 50

THE PENTATEUCH; Or the Five Books of Moses.
    School and Family Edition. By Rev. Drs. Adolph and Isaac Moses. CLOTH............................ 30

THE SOURCE OF ALL CIVILIZATION AND THE MEANS OF PRESERVING OUR CIVIL AND RELIGIOUS LIBERTY.
    By Rev. Dr. I. Kalish............................ 25

GUIDE FOR RATIONAL INQUIRIES INTO THE BIBLICAL WRITINGS. Being an examination of the doctrinal difference between *Judaism* and *Primitive Christianity*, based upon a critical exposition of the book of Matthew. 192 pages. By Rev. Dr. I. Kalish........................ 1 25

PHILOSOPHY AND PHILOSOPHICAL AUTHORS OF THE JEWS.
    A Historical Sketch, with explanatory notes. By S. Munk, Librarian of the National Library at Paris. Price..... 1 00

THREE NATIONAL LECTURES.
    I. Our Public Schools. II. Liberalism, its Nature and True End. III. Sacredness of Our Blessed Freedom. By Dr Mayer. Price for three lectures............................ 25

THE AMERICAN JEWISH PULPIT.
    A collection of sermons by the most eminent Rabbis of the United States. BOUND in CLOTH, full gilt.......... 2 00

BIBLE ETHICS.
    A manual of instruction in the history and principles of Judaism, according to the Hebrew Scriptures, by Revs. Jos. Krauskopf and Henry Berkowitz........ 50

ENGLISH SCHOOL AND FAMILY READER.
    For the use of Israelites. This book contains narrative and descriptive pieces, both poetry and prose; original, selected and translated from the Talmud; historical and biographical sketches of the great in Israel; scientific and instructive articles from the pens of the most prominent Jewish writers. By H. Abarbanel. 440 pp. 1 00

THE BLOCH PUB. AND PRINT. CO.,
Cincinnati, O.

THE AMERICAN HEBREW PUBLISHING HOUSE.

Any of the following publications will be sent postpaid to any address on receipt of affixed price.

BOOKS BY THE REV. DR. I. M. WISE.

HISTORY OF THE HEBREWS' FIRST COMMONWEALTH.
    A condensed history from Abraham to the destruction of Jerusalem .... $ 50

HISTORY OF THE HEBREWS' SECOND COMMONWEALTH.
    A compact narrative of Hebrew history from 536 B. C. E., to 70 C. E., arranged in a manner to assist the memory, and to make reading easy and pleasant. In CLOTH, $2; CLOTH, Gilt-edge, $2.50; MOROCCO, Full Gilt 3 00

JUDAISM.
    Its Doctrines and Duties. The most complete and concise compedium of Judaism from the rational standpoint 50

THE MARTYRDOM OF JESUS OF NAZARETH.
    PAPER, 75 cts.; CLOTH 1 00

THE COSMIC GOD.
    A book for thinkers and students. CLOTH 1 50

THREE LECTURES ON THE ORIGIN OF CHRISTIANITY.
    I. Jesus, the Pharisee. II. The Apostles and the Essenes. III. Paul and the Mystics. 35

JUDAISM AND CHRISTIANITY.
    Their Agreements and Disagreements. A course of popular lectures on Sinaic Revelation and Christian Theology 1 00

THE WANDERING JEW.
    A Lecture. The Jew of History as contrasted with the Jew of Fiction 25

MOSES, THE MAN AND STATESMAN.
    A Lecture 25

OUR COUNTRY'S PLACE IN HISTORY.
    A Lecture 10

TEMPERANCE QUESTION.
    An Essay. Read before the "Friends of Inquiry," Cincinnati, and showing wherein the fallacy and injustice of sumptuary laws exist 10

THE BLOCH PUB. AND PRINT. CO.,
Cincinnati, O.

www.ingramcontent.com/pod-product-compliance
Lightning Source LLC
Chambersburg PA
CBHW030342170426
43202CB00010B/1207